DATE DUE FOR RETURN

German Rococo: The Zimmermann Brothers

Henry-Russell Hitchcock

Allen Lane The Penguin Press London 1968

First published in 1968

Allen Lane The Penguin Press
Vigo Street London W1

Printed in Great Britain
by W & J Mackay & Co Ltd
Chatham Kent

Contents

Preface 7

List of Works 11

Text 15

Bibliographical Note 83

Plates following page 84

Notes on the Plates 85

Index 95

An meine deutschen Freunde,
insbesondere zu Düsseldorf

Preface

To turn from forty years' study of nineteenth- and twentieth-century architecture, particularly in the United States and Great Britain, and to offer a book on eighteenth-century Germany must seem somewhat presumptuous. In extenuation the author may plead that it is a small book, and that the literature on the subject in English has up until now been limited. Since Sacheverell Sitwell's introductory *German Baroque Art* of forty years ago there has appeared only a handful of books in English, four of them within the last decade, and all rather general in their coverage.* Dominikus Zimmermann has fared better than his contemporaries, however, since he has been the subject of a short article and even an unpublished thesis in English.

The situation is naturally very different as regards publications in German, for in Germany the national Baroque and Rococo have long been studied with scholarly assiduity. Both texts and collections of illustrations are not only multiple and profuse, they are still being produced in ever more generous format. Steinhausen and Die Wies, the principal works of the Zimmermanns, for example, have each been the subject of half-a-dozen or more books and pamphlets, the most complete concerning the latter appearing in 1964. Yet the only general account of Dominikus's work of any value came out first in a regional journal in Dillingen more than half a century ago, and that of his brother Johann Baptist has similarly been covered only in an earlier series of five articles in such another journal and an unpublished dissertation.

---

* But see the Bibliographical Note for the most important, Eberhard Hempel's, which appeared after this preface was written.

8

For long the study of Baroque architecture, whether Italian or non-Italian, was a German speciality. French scholars, refusing to accept that their own seventeenth-century architecture could be Baroque, except perhaps in spots, have only lately begun to take an interest in the subject. Within my own memory most Baroque architecture, both Italian and Northern, was still called 'Late Renaissance' by writers in English. As to the rather special problem of whether there was a German Rococo *architecture*, or merely an imported French style of interior *decoration* much used in buildings still generically Baroque, the issue has hardly existed except for German scholars. Fiske Kimball, the most serious American student of the Rococo, was if anything more chauvinistic than the French, recognizing little as significant in Germany except Cuvilliés's Amalienburg. If Nicolas Powell underlined the distinction by entitling his book *From Baroque to Rococo*, in the broad range of a somewhat hurried treatment he could not contribute to the subject much that was really new.

Nor can I hope to do so in this modest book, focused as it is on the work of only two men, although that work is here set against the background of period and region. Neither Dominikus nor Johann Baptist Zimmermann were Rococo artists when their careers began in the first decade of the eighteenth century. Yet, if their finest achievements, Steinhausen of 1728–33 and Die Wies of 1746–54, are still considered Late Baroque by many, it must at least be admitted that these contain, like the major churches of most other German architects of the second quarter of the eighteenth century, many Rococo elements. Whether one is justified in going further than that, the reader must judge from the text and illustrations that follow.

The written history of styles, including their definition and their morphology, is always controversial; moreover, it is generally less useful than study of the work of particular artists considered, if not timelessly, at least in their own particular contexts. Such very great architects as Michelangelo and Frank Lloyd Wright fit awkwardly into stylistic pigeon-holes, and those who concentrate their attention on problems of style usually find these men difficult to handle. Without necessarily going so far as to omit such figures entirely – as Gombrich did Ingres from his general history of European painting – some historians are tempted to distort their achievements on Procrustean beds of *a priori* categories and distinctions.

Rococo architecture, what it was or might have been, is but a subsidiary theme in this book. Elsewhere, I have returned to the problem.* Yet it is in this connection that the work of the

---

* Articles on the Asam brothers in the *Journal of the Society of*

Zimmermanns must be considered most characteristic of their age and land. At the least, a claim that they were essentially Rococo artists in their mature work – especially Johann Baptist – is less contentious than those sometimes made for the brothers C. D. and E. Q. Asam, for J. M. Fischer, or for J. B. Neumann. Dominikus's claim to be recognized as a major architect, moreover, is solider than François Cuvilliés's, although the latter's high international rank as a Rococo decorator has long been recognized – even by the French and by Kimball.

H.-R.H.

Architectural Historians in 1966; an article on the Schmuzers in the *Art Bulletin*; one on Peter Thumb in *Essays in the History of Architectture presented to Rudolf Wittkower*, both 1967; and *Rococo Architecture Studies* (1968), which includes these earlier articles as well as other material.

List of Works

Uncertain dates and doubtful attributions are queried (?); things no longer extant are bracketed.

J. B. Z.'s work in roman type.

D. Z.'s work in italics.

Character of work is indicated in parentheses.

(?)1706	[Tegernsee, Benedictine Monastery] (stucco)
1708	*Fischingen (Switzerland), Benedictine Abbey: Iddakapelle, high altar and four side altars (scagliola)*
1709–10	*Buxheim, Carthusian Monastery: Marienkapelle; Library; Sacristy; [Chapter house] (stucco)*
*1710	Edelstetten, Frauenstift Church (stucco, fresco)
1710	Waldsee, Augustinian Abbey Church: Sacristy (stucco, fresco)
*1710–11	Buxheim, Carthusian Monastery: Library; Sacristy (fresco)
*1711–12	*Buxheim, Carthusian Monastery Church (stucco, scagliola altars, fresco)*
1712	*Biberach, Pilgrimage Church: four side altars (scagliola)*
(?)1712–14	*Waldsee, Augustinian Abbey Church: high altar, Mariahilf altar (scagliola)*
1713	*Wemding, St-Emmeran: two side altars (scagliola)*
1714	Schliersee, Parish Church (stucco, fresco)
1714–19	Ottobeuren, Benedictine Abbey: Krankenkapelle;

*Illustrated.

	Chapter house; Refectory; Archive; etc. (stucco)
1715	*Birkland, Parish Church: high altar (scagliola)*
*1715–18	Ottobeuren, Benedictine Abbey: Library (stucco; scagliola)
1716	Freising, Cathedral: Cloister (stucco, fresco)
1716–17	[Ismaning, Schloss] (stucco, ? fresco)
*1716–21	*Mödingen, Dominican Nunnery Church (arch., stucco, fresco)*
1717	[Miesbach, Parish Church: side altar] (scagliola)
1718–19	*Ochsenhausen, Benedictine Abbey: Antonius-kapelle: altar (scagliola)*
*1718–20	*Landsberg, Rathaus: interiors; façade (stucco)*
1719	*Neresheim, Benedictine Abbey: Festsaal (stucco)*
(?)1720–25	Landsberg-am-Lech, Ursuline Nunnery Church (arch., stucco)
*1720–25	Schleissheim, Neues Schloss: Stairhall; [Maximiliankapelle]; Festsaal; Kammerkapelle; etc. (stucco)
*1720–29	*Mödingen, Dominican Nunnery (arch.)*
1721	*Kösingen, Parish Church: high altar (scagliola)*
1721	*Landsberg-am-Lech, Parish Church: Rosary altar (scagliola)*
1721–2	[*Würzburg, Neumünster: two side altars*] (*scagliola*); [two altarpieces] (oil)
1723–8	(?) Munich, Palais Preysing (stucco)
1724	*Würzburg, Neumünster: apse (scagliola, fresco),* [altarpiece] (oil)
1724–5	*Schwäbisch-Gmünd, Dominican Monastery Church (arch.)*
*1725	Benediktbeuern, Benedictine Abbey: Library (stucco, fresco)
1726	[Nymphenburg, Schloss: Electoral apartments] (stucco)
1726	Dietramzell, St Martin (stucco, fresco)
* (?)1726–7	*Buxheim, Parish Church (arch., stucco)*
1726–33	*Siessen, Dominican Nunnery Church (arch., stucco, fresco)*
1728	Tegernsee, Benedictine Monastery: Refectory (stucco, fresco)
1728–30	Munich, Residenz: Ahnengalerie (stucco)
*1728–33	*Steinhausen, Pilgrimage Church (arch., stucco, fresco)*
*1729	Weyarn, Augustinian Abbey Church (stucco, fresco)

* Illustrated.

1730	Beyharting, Augustinian Abbey Church (stucco, fresco)
1730	Emmering, Parish Church (fresco)
(?)1730–39	[Nymphenburg, Schloss: Chorfrauenkirche] (stucco)
*1731–2	Benediktbeuern, Benedictine Abbey: Neuer Festsaal (stucco, fresco)
1731–6	(?) Munich, Palais Porcia (stucco)
*1731–7	Munich, Residenz: Schatzkammer; Reiche Zimmer (stucco)
1732–4	[Würzburg, Neumünster: vaults (fresco); seven paintings] (oil)
*1732	*Project for Ottobeuren Abbey Church (arch.)*
1732	*Sankt Blasien, Benedictine Monastery: Marienkapelle, etc. (stucco)*
1733–7	(?)Munich, Palais Holnstein (stucco)
1733–9	*Buxheim, Carthusian Monastery: Cloister, etc. (arch.)*
1734	Seligenthal (Landshut), Cistercian Nunnery: Church (stucco, fresco)
1734	Vilgertshofen, Pilgrimage Church: choir (fresco)
*1734–9	Nymphenburg, Amalienburg (stucco)
1736	Nymphenburg, Badenburg: bath, frieze (stucco)
*1736–41	*Günzburg, Parish Church (arch.)*
1737	[Munich, St-Jakob-am-Anger] (stucco, fresco)
1737–8	Freising, Cathedral: Library (stucco)
*1738	Prien, Parish Church (stucco, fresco)
(?)1738	[Attel; Elandskapelle] (fresco)
*1738–40	*Buxheim, Carthusian Monastery: Annakapelle (arch; stucco)*; altar painting (oil)
1739	Hohenaschau, Schlosskapelle: side altar paintings (oil)
1740	[Würzburg, Neumünster: painting] (oil)
1740	[Ingolstadt, Franciscan Church] (fresco, ? stucco)
1741	*Project for Johanniskirche, Landsberg-am-Lech (arch.)*
1743–5	Berg-am-Laim (Munich), St-Michael (stucco, fresco)
1744–5	Dietramzell, Augustinian Abbey Church (stucco, fresco)
1745–54	(?) *Ingenried, Parish Church (arch.)*
*1746–54	*Die Wies, Pilgrimage Church (arch., stucco, fresco)*
1747–52	(?) Landshut, St-Blasius (arch.)

* Illustrated.

*1748–9	*Project for Premonstratensian Abbey of Schussenried (arch.)*
1748	Munich, Residenz, Hofkapelle: two side altars with paintings (stucco, oil)
1748	*Project for nave of Schongau Parish Church (arch.)*
1748	Markt Grafing, Dreifaltigkeitskirche (stucco, fresco)
1749	Landshut, St-Blasius (stucco, fresco)
(?)1750	*(?) Schwäbisch-Gmünd, Franziskanerkirche: altars (scagliola)*
*1750–52	*Landsberg-am-Lech, Johanniskirche (arch., scagliola)*
*1751–5	Andechs, Benedictine Abbey Church (? arch., stucco, fresco)
1752–3	[Munich, Residenz Theater, ceiling] (stucco)
1752–4	Wemding, Maria Brunnlein (stucco, fresco)
1753–6	[Munich, St-Peter: nave] (stucco, fresco)
1753–61	Munich-Harlaching, St-Anna (fresco)
1754	Margarethenberg: altar painting (oil)
*1754–6	Schäftlarn, Premonstratensian Abbey Church (stucco, fresco)
1754–63	*(?) Schussenried, Premonstratensian Abbey: Library*
*1755–63	*(?) Gutenzell, Cistercian Nunnery Church (arch.)*
1756	Freising, Neustift (stucco, fresco)
1756–7	*Eresing, Parish Church (arch.)*
*1755–7	Nymphenburg, Schloss: Festsaal, etc. (stucco, fresco)

* Illustrated.

Within the last generation, German architecture of the eighteenth century has come to be recognized internationally as a source of possible delight. In its profusion and in the quality of its finest achievements it rivals that of other highly esteemed periods elsewhere, even if hardly equal in historical significance to the French Gothic and the Italian Renaissance of which the justly exalted reputation was long ago established. Perhaps it is the contrast to the architecture of our own day, so scraped, so puritanical, and usually devoid of associated works of art of much intrinsic interest, that in part explains this appeal, an appeal that has developed outside Germany over the last forty years from amused, and even shocked, curiosity to real enthusiasm and warm admiration. In Germany affection for the national architecture of the previous century had already found expression, however dubiously, as early as the 1870s and 80s in the 'castles' built by Ludwig II of Bavaria. His Herrenchiemsee Schloss copies Versailles, of course, even to including a reconstruction of the long-destroyed *Escalier des ambassadeurs*; but several rooms there are decorated in highly theatrical imitation of the German Rococo, as is also true throughout his earlier Schloss at Linderhof. Serious historical study began also in the eighties.

The rather personal taste of the 'Mad King' became widely acceptable by the 1890s, in part thanks to books by scholars of repute, as innumerable ponderous public buildings of the period of William II make evident. Much later, in the 1920s, a more delicate Neo-Rococo provided a minor counter-current both to Expressionism and to the rising International Style, especially in the Berlin theatres of Oskar Kaufmann. The twenties saw also

several well-documented and handsomely-illustrated books devoted to eighteenth-century architecture in Germany. In that
decade, moreover, Sacheverell Sitwell first offered English readers
a fascinated, and fascinating, glimpse of German production in
his *German Baroque Art*, inferior though that book was to his
earlier *Southern Baroque Art*. Of the other books in English
devoted strictly to the subject, all have appeared within the last
decade (*see* Bibliographical Note). Evidence of the very considerable interest they have aroused is the fact that of at least one,
John Bourke's *Baroque Churches of Central Europe* of 1958, a
new edition was already required three years later.

Even so, though the great eighteenth-century German composers, Handel and Bach, are known to almost everyone, the
names of the architect Dominikus Zimmermann, born in the
same year 1685 as the two famous musicians, and of his five-years
older brother, the fresco-painter and stuccoist Johann Baptist
Zimmermann, are still relatively unfamiliar even to interested
English and American readers. Two slightly younger contemporaries, J. B. Neumann and J. M. Fischer, are certainly better
known; their names are more likely to evoke images of the
latter's great Benedictine abbey church at Ottobeuren and of the
former's vast palace at Würzburg, with its magnificent frescoes
by Tiepolo, unequalled even in Italy, than are the names of the
two Zimmermanns to bring up those of their masterpieces: Die
Wies, the sumptuous pilgrimage church on which both were
employed [Plates 39–45, 56–8], and the Amalienburg, where the
most highly reputed Rococo interiors outside France are decorated
with stuccoes executed by Johann Baptist for the architect
François Cuvilliés [Plates 25 and 26].

Die Wies and the Mirror Room in the Amalienburg are
perhaps the closest equivalents in the visual arts to the ecclesiastical and secular music of the leading German composers of the
day. Though Benedictines and even Premonstratensians may
sing Bach in our ecumenical day, I doubt that his Protestant
music was heard at Die Wies within his lifetime and that of
the brothers Zimmermann. The strains of Handel, moreover, must have been far more familiar at Hanover's Herrenhausen than at Bavaria's Nymphenburg; yet Carl Lamb, writing
in 1964 on Die Wies, did not hesitate to compare its interior with
Handel's 'Messiah', even though a taste for the music of Handel
developed in the Catholic south of Germany only in the late
eighteenth century, and in secular *milieux*.

However appropriate or inappropriate the Handelian analogy
may be, the Zimmermanns' artistic activity, extending through
a half-century from before 1710 nearly to 1760, was certainly
integral to a period of great brilliance in German architecture,

the most brilliant since the *Sondergotik* of the late Middle Ages, if not indeed the Romanesque. Eighteenth-century German architectural production, moreover, unlike musical composition, centred in the Catholic south: in Upper Bavaria between the Alps and the Danube, in Franconia and the Upper Palatinate north of the Danube – all three included in the present Bavarian State – and in Swabia, partly along the western edge of Bavaria and partly in what is now the State of Baden-Württemberg. Outside this region the close family connections of various prelates and lay rulers with the Bavarian and Franconian princes led to a sparser extension still farther westward in various districts running up the Rhine from Düsseldorf to the Lake of Constance and even in Westphalia.

Such periods of intense architectural activity and achievement, restricted in time to four or five decades and often to some particular portion only of a modern nation, are not unfamiliar: Attica in the fifth century B.C., the Île-de-France in the twelfth century, and Tuscany in the fifteenth are the most famous instances from the earlier past. In this portion of the eighteenth century somewhat comparable centres can be recognized in Piedmont in Italy, once more in Paris and the Île-de-France, but most familiarly for Anglo-Saxons in the England of George II. There the Burlingtonian 'Rule of Taste' coincided almost exactly in date with the ascendance of the Rococo in France and Germany.

The Bavarian *Blütezeit* was quite different from the French Gothic, the Florentine Renaissance, and the English Georgian which are often further described as 'Early'. The twelfth-century Gothic of the Île-de-France and the Renaissance in *quattrocento* Tuscany were initiatory stages in what later became international movements of great vigour and very long duration. Even the short-lived Anglo-Palladian of eighteenth-century England can be considered not improperly a sort of transition between the international Late Baroque and international Romantic Classicism. But the German florescence, like the Rococo in France, had no related sequel.

Statistics have little value in the history of architecture since great periods are usually distinguished not so much by the quantity as by the quality of their production. Yet Max Hauttman's considered estimate, given in his *Geschichte der kirchlichen Baukunst in Bayern, Schwaben und Franken 1550–1780* of 1921, that between 1700 and 1780 two hundred churches of some artistic importance were built in this area is not without significance, at least in contrast to his figure of considerably less than a hundred for the previous 120 years, blighted for more than a generation by the Thirty Years' War and its aftermath.

Periods of intense creative activity are not necessarily associated with historical situations in which new social forces and major economic developments are rapidly changing the traditional scene, much less with violent political upheavals. The revolutionary period in French eighteenth-century architecture preceded rather than followed the political revolution; the revolutions of the twentieth century have hardly been more productive of great architecture than the counter-revolutions. It need not be considered a paradox, therefore, that political and social conditions in eighteenth-century Germany, when so many great buildings – and especially churches – were erected and decorated, seem to have been anything but advanced, and the period ended well before the Industrial Revolution began at all to influence the Continent. Eighteenth-century Europe was not usually at its best in building churches. But German piety continued to be medieval, both in intensity and in artistic productivity, and German rulers were in more absolute control of their petty states than ever before.

The political and social situation in eighteenth-century Germany merits some further description. Down to the French Revolution, which did not affect this part of Europe until a generation after the Zimmermanns' careers came to an end, the lands with which we are concerned continued to constitute a rather considerable part of that grandiose anachronism, the Holy Roman Empire, founded a thousand years earlier by Charlemagne and long headed by the Habsburgs in Vienna. In the early eighteenth century, however, the principal German rulers were, in fact, the few princes who were Electors of the Empire, not the Emperor. Six electorates were hereditary; the others were held by a special sort of ecclesiastic, prince-bishops, although only three of the many German prince-bishops were electors.

An exact figure for the number of German prince-bishops is hard to give, since several of the bishoprics of the Empire, Liège, Trent and Strasbourg, if not perhaps Salzburg, lie outside what almost anyone but Pan-Germans would now consider German territory. But some fifteen or sixteen of them, controlling territories with perhaps two million inhabitants, must also be ranked as among the real rulers of eighteenth-century Germany. There were in addition three prince-abbots and one prince-prior: of Kempten, Berchtesgaden, Corvey; and of Ellwangen. Thus, as in the Middle Ages, so still in the 1700s the Church through various semi-secular manifestations was a major political as well as a religious power – not for nothing was this 'Roman' Empire also called 'Holy'. This ignores, however, thirty to forty princes who were not electors (though some of them, such as the Prince of Waldeck and Pyrmont, ruled territories of considerable extent and built accordingly); innumerable 'imperial counts'; many prelates who were not princes; and some fifty 'free towns' of which three, Hamburg, Bremen and Lübeck, survive as such even today.

Of the two princely families that provided a very great part of the architectural patronage in southern Germany in the period of the Zimmermanns' activity, the Wittelsbachs and the Schönborns, the most important Wittelsbachs were laymen, but the almost equally powerful Schönborns were all ecclesiastics. These two families held between them more than half of the electorates. The electors of Bavaria, as also the electors Palatine and the electors of Cologne, were Wittelsbachs. Through most of this period Schönborns were prince-bishops of Bamberg and of Würzburg as well as dukes in Franconia; while along the Rhine they were archbishops or bishops of Mainz, of Speyer and Constance, and of Worms and Trier. The archbishops of Trier and of Mainz were also electors. According to the same pattern, the Elector of Cologne was the archbishop. The Schönborn Elector of Trier, Franz Georg, became also prince-prior of Ellwangen. The elector of Mainz, Lothar Franz von Schönborn, not only ruled large territories eastward in Franconia as prince-bishop of Bamberg but was in addition prince-primate and arch-chancellor of the Empire; his nephew, Friedrich Carl, who became bishop of Würzburg as well as of Bamberg, had earlier been vice-chancellor and then lived in Austria. These imperial dignities help to explain the artistic connections with Vienna evident in the patronage of the Schönborns in their German lands, connections that differentiate them from the Wittelsbachs. The latter were usually closer to France culturally as well as politically and by marriage. However, the Bavarian Elector Carl Albrecht was actually Emperor as Karl VII for a few years in the 1740s at the expense of being driven out of Bavaria by Maria Theresia's Austrian troops, as his father had been earlier in the century, by her father's troops.

Such statements necessarily simplify drastically a complicated pattern that changed with the years; nor can one readily explain how, or why, prince-bishoprics, including ecclesiastical electorates, descended so often from uncle to nephew almost as automatically as did lay-electorates from father to son, or at least to the nearest male heir. But what has been said does not exaggerate the concentration of power, and hence of architectural patronage, in the hands of a very few families. Hardly more than the two mentioned are of much consequence in this period in south-eastern Germany, although there were from time to time prince-bishops of Bamberg and of Würzburg who were not Schönborns. Moreover, the power of these families was not restricted to the south-east. One Wittelsbach, Clemens August, son and brother of Bavarian electors, was already from 1719 prince-bishop of Münster and Paderborn, from 1724 of Hildesheim, and from 1728 of Osnabrück, as well as archbishop and elector of Cologne in succession to his Wittelsbach uncle, Joseph Clemens, from 1723. Thus his realm eventually extended north-eastward beyond the duchy of Berg, held by the Wittelsbach elector Palatine, across much of what is now the state of North Rhine–Westphalia – the industrial heart of modern Germany, but of much less significance economically in the eighteenth century – all the way into present-day Lower Saxony. From 1732, as grand-master of the Deutsch Orden in succession to another Wittelsbach, Clemens August had further opportunities to build, especially at Mergentheim (now Bad Mergentheim) in Württemberg, the headquarters of the order, and at Ellingen in Franconia, a region otherwise dominated by the Schönborns.

In addition to the prince-bishops among churchly patrons of architecture were the heads of the great abbeys and convents whose arms are usually proudly displayed on the great works they undertook. Indeed, they concerned themselves far more with new church-building and with the redecoration of older churches in this period, not to speak of the reconstruction of their monasteries, than did the prince-bishops. Such activities over-shadowed in southern Germany even the palace-building in which the electoral princes, both lay and religious, were chiefly interested. It was they, moreover, who took charge of erecting and decorating the principal new pilgrimage churches (see p. 24). These abbots and priors, abbesses and prioresses were often not of princely origin, even though four were *ex-officio* prince-prelates, but they were among the actual German rulers of the period. Moreover, many of their monasteries disposed of means – or at least were ready to use them – relatively greater than in the Middle Ages when most of the vast monastic estates had been established by grants and legacies, and their big churches first built. One or other of the Zimmermanns, for example, worked at various times for Carthusians, Dominicans, Cistercians, Augustinians and for Dominican, Cistercian and Ursuline nuns; but in their major commissions both served principally in the Benedictines and the Premonstratensians.

The sources of the funds of magnates other than heads of monasteries and nunneries – electors, other lay-princes, and prince-bishops – were their own personal estates and, in addi-tion, the total of the income-producing taxes, tolls, and so forth imposed in their territories. Little or no distinction was made between the purse of the ruler and the treasury of the state he ruled – often no larger than the land-holdings of contemporary British magnates, and probably at this time not even so productive. The great wealth of many of the south German abbeys in the eighteenth century, the wealth which paid for their multifarious building activities, seems – and, indeed, was as regards most of the Old World if not the New – an anachronism. In England the holdings of the monasteries had already been distributed in the sixteenth century. By this time there existed no comparable reservoirs of ecclesiastical wealth – drained in southern Germany only with the general secularization of 1803 in the Napoleonic period – in the Protestant north of Europe, including north Germany.

German monasteries had been hard hit in the seventeenth century by the Thirty Years' War. But campaigns of physical repair and reconstruction had already been underway for two full generations when the Zimmermanns came on the scene around 1710. By the early eighteenth century the monasteries had evidently had plenty of time in which to put their estates in order, even though serious improvement in agricultural methods, already significant in Holland, hardly reached southern Germany within the period under consideration. Even in England such improvement came chiefly after the mid-century. Yet well before that large land-owners could, and did, accumulate very considerable wealth in Great Britain – often, as in the case of some German monasteries, thanks to the exploitation of minerals below the soil. The wealth that in England went so often into 'country houses', the great rural mansions built by the Whig aristocracy under George II, went in south Germany in large part, of course, to the lay-rulers, big and little, but in relatively great proportion still to the monasteries.

The large and medium-sized *Schlösser* the prince-bishops built away from cities, as at Pommersfelden, Bruchsal and Werneck among the Schönborn seats and at Brühl, Herzogsfreude, Clemenswerth and Liebenburg among those of just one Wittelsbach, Clemens August, elector of Cologne, are comparable rather to the more elaborate English country houses and French châteaux of the day than to the vast Versailles palace of Louis XIV that several especially ambitious German princes had been attempting for a generation to emulate. But modest country houses, such as abound in England, were not so often built in this period when the minor nobility, as in the France of Louis XIV, preferred to haunt the courts of the princes and usually left the management of their estates to agents.

The Zimmermanns and other leading architects and decorators worked only very occasionally on, or at, such smaller houses. Johann Baptist was employed at Ismaning, a minor seat near Munich of the bishop of Freising; just possibly at Alteglofsheim near Regensburg for Count von Königsfeld, who was a prominent figure at the Munich electoral court; and in the chapel of the medieval Schloss Hohenaschau of the Preysings, for whose new-built mansions of the period in Munich he probably also provided the stucco-work. Dominikus built only the free-standing chapel at Schloss Pöring near Landsberg for Joseph Marquard von Berntoff, though that served also as a very modest pilgrimage church. These are all rather unimportant additions to inconsiderable houses, usually of much earlier date, in evident contrast to the big and sumptuous new churches, monasteries, and palace-interiors of the period.

Not only was the south German scene still largely medieval in its more positive social aspects, so was it also – and early medieval at that – in a negative way. The rise of the middle class, a continuing rise characteristically expressed in eighteenth-century England, and even in the France of the *ancien régime*, by the prominence, as patrons, of men of that class who were buying their way into the aristocracy partly by architectural display, was hardly of importance in Germany. In fact Germans of the middle class were on the whole building less, and less handsomely, than in the later Middle Ages and the Renaissance. Bamberg and Augsburg – which was now only half as large a city as in the sixteenth century – have some new merchants' mansions; but Munich has more nobles' palaces such as those of the Preysings. In Munich, however, two surviving architects' houses, that of E. Q. Asam (1692–1750) beside the church that he built in the Sendingstrasse in the 1730s, a medieval structure with the façade disguised by very rich Rococo stucco decoration, and the more modest one of J. B. Gunetzrhainer (1692–1765), from 1745 electoral *Oberhofbaumeister* (principal court-architect), in the Promenadeplatz are of real interest.

Such important new Rhineland cities as the Margrave of Baden-Durlach's Karlsruhe and the elector palatine's Mannheim were growing outward from the palaces of their princes, initiated respectively in 1715 and 1720, just as Rastatt near Baden-Baden and Ludwigsburg in Württemberg had begun to do somewhat earlier. But these and more modest examples such as the Prince of Waldeck and Pyrmont's Arolsen, begun in 1711, were *fiat*-towns like Versailles. They had little of the oligarchical character of the London West End of the Georgian period or the St-Germain quarter of Paris, not to speak of the ranges of great seventeenth- and eighteenth-century merchants' houses that line the canals in Amsterdam and are also found even in the smaller Dutch cities. Late and exceptional is the Schäzler Haus in Augsburg of 1765–7 by Cuvilliés's follower C. A. von Lespilliez (1723–96) in which the saloon rivals the greatest palace interiors of the previous half century. The client here was the banker Liebert, heir in function though not in fact to the sixteenth-century Fuggers. Unless, indeed, J. B. Zimmermann provided (as is rather doubtful) the stucco-work on the Patrizier Kern at Wasserburg-am-Inn, like the Asam Haus in Munich a pair of medieval façades redecorated, it would appear that he had no middle-class clients, except in so far as some of the heads of the monasteries for which he worked may have been of middle-class — indeed, even of peasant — origin.

Civic buildings are few and usually modest compared to those of earlier periods in the same region. The eighteenth century has nothing to offer equal to Elias Holl's Rathaus of a hundred years earlier in Augsburg. Such buildings, moreover, were often princely benefactions rather than manifestations of civic wealth and power. The one at Bonn was built by Michel Léveilly (†1762) for Clemens August, whose principal seat was there, in 1737–8; that at Ellingen — not in fact originally a Rathaus — in 1744 by F. J. Roth for the Deutsch Orden, whose Grand Master then was none other than that same Wittelsbach potentate. However, in 1718–20, Dominikus Zimmermann decorated first the inside and then the outside of the Rathaus at Landsberg-am-Lech in Upper Bavaria for the town council [Plate 7]. (He had been for two years a citizen of Landsberg, and in 1734 became himself a member of the council; still later he was mayor.)

One of Dominikus's three major works, the parish church at Günzburg [Plates 29–34], a Swabian town under direct Imperial control, was commissioned in June, 1736, by the town council. But, after the *détente* of the early 1740s during the War of the Austrian Succession, it took the contributions of various individual donors to complete the furnishing twenty years later. Dominikus's remodelling in 1756–7 of the Eresing parish church near Landsberg, partly fifteenth century and partly seventeenth century, was perhaps undertaken in this small village for the parish priest, as may also have been true of the new parish church at Ingenried near Kaufbeuren begun in 1745. The cornerstone there, however, was laid by the Abbot of Steingaden, Dominikus's client for his great church at Die Wies. Yet funds were evidently very limited, even though they were probably provided in part by the monks of Steingaden, and the result is so pathetic it is hard to accept that even the original design was his. Much superior is the parish church at Schongau, nearer Steingaden, for whose nave Dominikus prepared a design in 1748 that has survived; but Franz Xaver II Schmuzer (1713–75), or some other stuccoist not yet identified, made various modifications while executing it in 1750–3.

Such modest early commissions for scagliola altars as Dominikus carried out at Wemding in 1713 and at Birkland in 1715, as also at Kösingen even later in 1721, where his three-part altar fills the whole east end of the tiny interior, were for parish churches where the client may have been the local 'lord of the manor', the priest, or some monastery – at Kösingen it was the nearby Benedictine abbey of Neresheim, where Dominikus had decorated the Festsaal in 1719. Often the control was in the hands of some great prelate: most of the parish churches designed by J. B. Neumann (1687–1753), for example, were built for one or another Schönborn. Except for J. B. Zimmermann's work of 1758 at Prien on the Chiemsee [Plates 27 and 28], however, and of course Dominikus's church at Günzburg, such things are the trivia of the Zimmermannian canon and can well be ignored. Dominikus's two other major works, on both of which his brother collaborated, Steinhausen [Plates 13–20] and Die Wies [Plates 39–45, 56–8], are pilgrimage churches.

These are a special sort of shrine, very often in eighteenth-century Germany of great size and magnificence, built to house some work of art or relic that provided a focus of intense devotion as a result of miraculous cures and other evidences of grace. Rising floods of pilgrims – floods still continuing today – created as in the Middle Ages the need for such new churches. The generous contributions of the pilgrims provided, as still in the case of modern ones like that of Fatimà in Portugal or Le Corbusier's Notre-Dame-du-Haut at Ronchamp in France, most of the requisite funds. In the twentieth century the architectural distinction of pilgrimage churches seems to be in inverse propor-tion to their size and cost – certainly in the case of the two just mentioned. But in eighteenth-century Germany the monasteries that cared for these shrines and usually hired the best architects to build them were more than ready to outshine their own churches – for example at Steinhausen in south-western Swabia where the client was the Premonstratensian abbot of nearby Schussenried, and at Die Wies in Upper Bavaria, which was administered by the Premonstratensians of Steingaden. Domini-kus's design of 1748 for a new church at Schussenried, made while his son Georg was a monk there, never came to execution; and his project for the associated monastery was only carried out over the years 1752–70 in much reduced form by his former assistant Jakob Emele (1706–80). At Steingaden the choir of the medieval church had been vaulted and decorated in the 1660s; only the vaulted ceiling of the nave and its decoration with stuccoes by Franz Xaver II Schmuzer (1713–75) and frescoes by J. G. Bergmüller (1688–1762) date from 1740–51, shortly before and during the construction and decoration of the very costly new church at Die Wies.

If churches make up almost the whole of Dominikus Zimmermann's production, as for that matter of such other leading Bavarian and Franconian architects of the day as J. M. Fischer (1692–1766), the brothers C. D. and E. Q. Asam and, to a rather lesser extent, J. B. Neumann (1687–1753), the second important contemporary field of activity was, as in the Renaissance, palace-building. Many palaces, however, had been begun in the late seventeenth century: Nymphenburg, for example, in 1663 and Schleissheim in 1684, to name two Wittelsbach seats near Munich, at which J. B. Zimmermann would be working in the 1720s [Plates 8 and 9], 30s [Plates 25 and 26] and 50s [Plates 53 and 54]. But it was in these decades that they received from Zimmermann and others most of their rich interior decoration in stucco and fresco as well as notable accessory buildings.

Despite the vast amount of production and the great size of many individual projects – the Ludwigsburg and Mannheim palaces intentionally rivalled Versailles in extent, while Ottobeuren has been called the Swabian Escorial – it is the interior architecture of the period that is most characteristic and distinguished. The principal architectural works were the big churches with their rich stucco decoration and extensive cycles of fresco painting overhead. These, moreover, are truly examples of interior *architecture*, not as in the case of most of the finest French, much English, and a great deal of German secular work of the day merely examples of interior *decoration*. Somewhere in between come the larger rooms of the palaces and monasteries, the stairhalls and the saloons, often at least as monumental as medium-sized churches. These are especially associated with Neumann, although J. B. Zimmermann also contributed notably to the creation of such interiors: early under Josef Effner (1687–1745) at Schleissheim in 1720–24 [Plate 8] and later, in association with François Cuvilliés (1695–1768) at Nymphenburg in 1756–7 [Plate 53].

To this middle range belong also several of the libraries in the monasteries. This is not so true of the early one at Ottobeuren where J. B. Zimmermann worked in 1715–18 [Plate 4], much less of Dominikus's at Buxheim, just outside Memmingen, of 1710, or those at Benediktbeuern, near Bad Tölz, of 1722–5 [Plate 10] and at Freising Cathedral of 1732–8. In these, however, Johann Baptist's decorations were restricted to the ceilings of rooms of modest height and conventional rectangular shape with little or no spatial interest. Even in the Austrian monasteries the grandest and most famous libraries are relatively late: that by Jakob Prandtauer (1660–1726) at Melk was completed after his death by Josef Mungennast (1720–85) in 1728; while Mungennast's at Altenburg is of 1740, and Gotthart Hayberger's at Sankt

Florian and at Admont are of 1744 and 1745. The rooms of this sort that Johann Baptist decorated were constructed, not by leading architects like Prandtauer, but by obscure men associated with the respective monasteries. The library at Schussenried, presumably projected by Dominikus in 1748 but certainly executed only after 1752 by Emele, is in a quite different class. So also are the even handsomer early one by Christian Wiedemann (1680–1739) and his son Johann (†1773) of 1738–44 at Wiblingen outside Ulm and that at Sankt Peter in the Black Forest, begun in the mid-1730s by Peter II Thumb (1681–1766) and decorated after 1750, not to speak of the library which Thumb began in 1757 at Sankt Gallen in Switzerland. Considerable absolute size; height emphasized and rectangular shape modified by swinging galleries round the walls – as indeed already rather primly at Ottobeuren – large ceiling frescoes, rich stucco decoration and even statuary, together with furnishings almost as elaborate as in contemporary churches: these features make such libraries among the most generally admired works of the mid-century when the German Rococo was at its height.

The question as to what this monumental German interior architecture should be called, whether Late Baroque or Rococo, has long troubled historians of art, especially as certain German scholars have considered the two terms almost synonymous. In its large scale and in some other architectonic qualities this German interior architecture of the middle decades of the century has, as is to be expected, a good deal in common with German ecclesiastical and palace architecture of the previous half century. That architecture of the decades just before and just after 1700 is quite properly considered Baroque since it follows closely the Early Baroque of Italy and, indeed, was often the work of Italian or Italian–Swiss artists. Then, rather belatedly, the bolder German designers began to draw upon the Roman High Baroque of Bernini and Borromini. This the Asam brothers, at least, knew at first hand and emulated with great success at Weltenburg, on the Danube above Regensburg, in 1716–21. In German lands as distinguished from Bohemia, rather less than is often supposed derives from the Piedmontese Baroque of Guarini, even though that had become available for study and emulation in published engravings as early as 1686. (The posthumous publication of Guarini's work by Vittone in the *Architettura civile* of 1737 was too late to be very influential.)

The profuse decoration modelled in stucco, even though of a character increasingly bolder than that of the delicate ornamentation of the French Rococo, owes much of its idiosyncratic character even as early as the 1720s, and still more from the mid-30s, not to Italy but to France. Despite the change in material from carved woodwork – commonly used for wall decoration in eighteenth-century France and also in many German palace interiors of modest size and for minor church fittings such as choir-stalls and confessionals – to moulded stucco, often in fairly high relief, and the associated modulation from delicate laciness to fully architectural scale, the resultant ensembles are quite different from the Italian Baroque, even of this very late date, and even more different from the sturdy German Baroque as still seen in such a great church as the Cathedral of Fulda built by Johann Dientzenhofer (1665–1726) in the opening decade of the century (1705–12). But if the larger German interiors in churches and palaces that were carried out in the 1730s, 40s and 50s be considered as examples of Rococo *architecture* – and Die Wies [Plates 42–5] has been so considered almost as generally as the Amalienburg interiors [Plates 25 and 26] have been accepted as prime examples of Rococo interior decoration – one must also concede that they are very remote from the Rococo as understood in France in the eighteenth century, or by such a modern historian of art as Fiske Kimball.

Especially characteristic of this stylistic ambiguity is the prominence of large-scale fresco painting, a feature certainly more Baroque than Rococo and more Italian than French. Not unknown in the late seventeenth century, this had been much further developed in Germany in the second decade of the century by Italians such as the Venice-trained Neapolitan Jacopo Amigoni (1675–1752) and by northerners who had studied in Rome or in Vienna, where the leading Roman master of aerial perspective, Andrea Pozzo (1642–1709), who had been born in Trent, worked after 1702. (Moreover, a German translation of Pozzo's treatise *Perspectivae pictorum* was brought out at Augsburg in two volumes in 1706–9.) Some of the finest monumental German interiors of this period, however, are without ceiling frescoes. Especially notable are Neumann's Weisser Saal in the Würzburg Residenz, with stucco decoration of 1744 by the Swiss Antonio Bossi (†1764) from the Ticino, and the chapel in Schloss Werneck, completed the next year by the same team. But the Weisser Saal is flanked by two much larger rooms, the saloon (Kaisersaal) and the stairhall, in which the frescoed ceilings by G. B. Tiepolo of the early fifties are often considered the finest – as that in the stairhall is the largest – executed anywhere in the eighteenth century. A project of the early forties for the stairhall, once preserved in the Staatliche Kunstbibliotek in Berlin, nevertheless indicates that at that point Neumann intended no fresco on the ceiling but only Rococo decoration in stucco, presumably by Bossi, as in the Weisser Saal.

Such vast frescoes as Italians before Tiepolo painted in

Germany and the very much greater number of them by J. B. Zimmermann and various Austrians, Swiss, and other Germans have few extant counterparts in interiors of the eighteenth century in France – LeMoyne's of 1733–6 in the Salon d'Hercule at Versailles is very exceptional, and Coypel's of 1710 in the Versailles chapel was, unlike the architectural scheme of this influential interior, rarely emulated in French churches. Uninfluenced – indeed definitely disapproved – by Paris, these overhead frescoes continued in Germany an Italian tradition that goes back to Pietro da Cortona's palace-ceilings in Rome and Florence of a century earlier and even to Correggio and Mantegna. In Bavaria, where they were still something of a novelty in the early eighteenth century, their incorporation in what may be called 'proto-Rococo' interiors of the early 1720s such as that at Aldersbach near Passau, those at Schleissheim [Plate 8], and in the redecoration of Freising Cathedral, required the services of the Italian Amigoni or the Rome-trained C. D. Asam. French Rococo influence, however, was already having some effect on the decorations at Schleissheim, thanks to the decade that Max Emanuel, the Bavarian Elector, and his architect Effner had spent in France, and was almost at once at least faintly reflected in the stucco-work of the Asams' church interiors. An electoral order of 1720 stated, on the other hand, in a characteristic mixture of tongues, that the painting in Bavarian churches should conform to the standards of the 'grosse Maîtres der Italiener'.

At Pommersfelden near Bamberg in Franconia in the stairhall and the saloon (Marmorsaal) of Schloss Weissenstein the Swiss J. R. Byss (1660–1738) and the Bavarian J. F. M. Rottmayr (c. 1655–1730), respectively – both Italian-trained and already prominent in Vienna – had in 1717 painted such ceilings for Lothar Franz von Schönborn, Elector of Mainz and arch-chancellor of the Empire, on the recommendation of his nephew the vice-chancellor in Vienna and, presumably, of the nephew's Genoa-born architect Johann Lukas von Hildebrandt (1668–1745). On the other hand, after French influence became still stronger in Munich towards 1730 than in the early twenties, on account of the years of training in Paris from which Max Emanuel's Walloon-born protégé Cuvilliés had profited, no large ceiling frescoes were used in the interiors that Cuvilliés carried out for the next elector, Carl Albrecht. There are, however, small paintings executed in oil by B. A. Albrecht (1687–1765) set into the vault of the Gallery of Ancestors (Ahnengalerie) in the Munich Residenz, presumably at the behest of Effner rather than of Cuvilliés, dating from the late twenties. Moreover, before their wartime destruction, there were also modest ceiling vignettes by

Albrecht in Cuvilliés's Grüne Galerie of 1733 in the Residenz. Large secular ceiling frescoes reappeared in this *milieu* only much later when J. B. Zimmermann and his son painted those in the Nymphenburg Great Hall and associated rooms [Plate 53] in the mid-fifties for the Elector Max III Joseph, still under Cuvilliés's direction.

It was doubtless Neumann's close links with Paris, beginning with a visit there in 1723, that led him often to eschew these most prominent features of monumental eighteenth-century interiors in Germany. Yet, as has already been noted, he did not miss the ultimate opportunity in the years just preceding his death in 1753 to collaborate in the Kaisersaal at Würzburg with Tiepolo, the greatest fresco-painter of the age, and produce there an interior that is essentially more Late Baroque than Rococo, but a masterpiece however it is labelled. Elsewhere than at Würzburg Neumann had not always been so fortunate in his painter-collaborators. One may well prefer the unfrescoed interior of the Werneck chapel, with its rich Rococo stucco-work by Bossi, or that of Neumann's early Benedictine priory church at Holz-kirchen of 1728–30, where the stucco decoration by J. P. Castelli (who had worked for Boffrand at Würzburg in 1724) is of almost French delicacy, to those with painted ceilings such as St-Paulinus in Trier and Heusenstamm, both frescoed by C. T. Scheffler (1699–1756) in the early forties. This subject must be considered again later, and with some attention to the illusionistic character of the frescoes and their resultant spatial effect, in discussing the major works of the Zimmermanns, Steinhausen and Die Wies; for in those churches the ceiling frescoes of Johann Baptist [Plates 19 and 44] play a truly archi-tectural role and must surely have been planned in close consul-tation with the architect, his brother.

One of the most conspicuous aspects of the large-scale building of this period, the profusion of stucco-work, has led many critics to consider even the grandest interiors primarily as examples of decoration, itself specifically if provincially Rococo, yet all but devoid of novel architectonic qualities that would differentiate them as Rococo architecture from the generic Baroque. Yet German interior architecture of the mid-eighteenth century can hardly be justly considered apart from its characteristic decora-tion. Where an interior must be seen naked without stucco-work as in Neumann's Etwashausen chapel outside Kitzingen of 1740–45, the very peak of the Rococo period, one must admit that little if anything distinctly non-Baroque or definably Rococo is recognizable.

It is natural and proper that we should apprehend mid-eighteenth-century churches in the form in which they have usually come down to us: complex works of art almost unimaginable without their full complement, not only of stucco decoration and frescoes, but also of rich altars, pulpits, choir-stalls, organ-cases and confessionals. The actual dates of execution of these accessories, which may well seem to the casual eye quite homogeneous in style with the ceiling decorations, often reveal that their roster includes items ten, twenty, thirty, or even forty years posterior in date to the original construction. In many cases the total effect of the interior is, therefore, much more distinctly or intensely Rococo than it would have been when these churches were new and still unfurnished, especially if they were built before the mid-thirties – provided, that is, none of the conspicuous fittings are later than about 1770. The high altar of 1779, for example, so distinctly post-Rococo in its stiff rectangularity, is a most unfortunate intrusion in Neumann's exquisite Kapelle at Würzburg of 1747–52, and the absence of the original high altar (it was destroyed in 1872 when the church was brutally restored) in Dominikus Zimmermann's Siessen, even though it dated from 1762–3, thirty years after the church was consecrated, unbalances the whole interior by leaving a focal void as is even more disturbing in the handsome rotunda of Herrgottsruh near Augsburg as decorated by C. D. Asam (1686–1739) and F. X. I. Feuchtmayr (1705–64) in the late thirties.

There can be, all the same, a real dichotomy in eighteenth-century German interiors, and in several of the grandest and most gorgeous this can be almost uncomfortably obvious. The greatest churches of J. M. Fischer's maturity, although extremely impressive externally in a still very Baroque way – Zwiefalten, Fürstenzell and Ottobeuren, both in Swabia – are, as regards the particular sort of architectonic expression at which Fischer (1692–1766) seems to have been aiming, all but overwhelmed in their interiors by the profuse Rococo decoration which is, in any case, quite considerably later in date.

Peculiarly characteristic of the situation, and undoubtedly conducive to the Zimmermanns' great artistic success with the range of means at the disposal of eighteenth-century south German churchbuilders, was the fact that both of them, like Joseph Schmuzer (1683–1753) and unlike Fischer and Neumann among their close contemporaries, began as stucco-workers. Dominikus, moreover, in his early years from 1708 – the date of his first identified work – to the mid-twenties, was even more a specialist in the design and execution of altars in the coloured and polished scagliola Germans call *Stuckmarmor*. Though he rarely painted in fresco – perhaps only once in his mature years (pp. 66–7) – he was certainly also responsible directly or indirectly for a good deal of figure-work in stucco. There was a specific payment to him in

1730 for the Apostles atop the piers at Steinhausen [Plates 17–19], and putti are frequently included in his decorative schemes [Plates 36, 42 and 43]. After the building of his modest and quite dull first church at Mödingen in 1716–18 [Plate 5], however, he was more and more concerned with full-scale architectural design: thus he became a conductor, so to say, of the contemporary artistic orchestra rather than merely a soloist.

Johann Baptist had from the first included small frescoed medallions, at least, in his stucco-work. One of his earliest signed works, the sacristy ceiling at Waldsee in southern Württemberg, dated 1710, has in the centre a relatively large fresco of the Last Supper that is of better quality – certainly more clearly visible – than those of about the same date set much higher over-head at Edelstetten, near Kumbach, or at Buxheim [Plates 1 and 3]. But the commission for the large fresco associated with his stucco decorations on the ceiling of the Ottobeuren library [Plate 4] went as late as 1717 to the obscure, but then better established, Elias Zobel, a Salzburger who had been active earlier in Prague. (Zobel had already supplied the modest frescoes incorporated in Zimmermann's other stuccoed ceilings in the monastery, several of which were initiated three years or so before that in the library.) Johann Baptist's really significant achievement in the field of large-scale painting – the score or so of oil-painted altarpieces, etc., identified as by him can be disregarded here – began with the frescoes of 1725 incorporated in the stucco-work of his library ceiling at Benediktbeuern [Plate 10]. In them the happy result of his association in 1720–24 with C. D. Asam and Amigoni in the stairhall, the Maximiliankappele, and the Festsaal at Schleissheim [Plate 8] becomes apparent (see pp. 40–44).

Should J. B. Zimmermann, stuccoist and fresco-painter, also be considered to have been an architect? He was never specifically employed as such. But of much of his early work one may properly say that there is little intrinsic interest in the buildings themselves, which are at least nominally designed by such minor figures as the Benedictine Father Christoph Vogt (1648–1725) at Edelstetten in 1709–10, and presumably also at Ottobeuren in 1714–18, and by Michael Ötschmann (1670–1755) at Benedikt-beuern in 1724–5 and 1731–2. It is Zimmermann's stucco-work and, beginning with the Benediktbeuern library, his frescoes that give these interiors their considerable artistic value [Plates 1, 4, 10 and 23].

Rather later, at Prien in 1738, Johann Baptist decorated the parish church [Plates 27 and 28], begun in 1735 by the local architect Johann Steinpeisz (see p. 66). Then, in 1744–5, that at Dietramzell – where he had worked in the parish church much earlier – he stuccoed and frescoed the Augustinian abbey church not far from Bad Tölz rebuilt in 1729–41 by an unrecorded architect; and, still later, the pilgrimage church of Maria Brünnlein outside the town of Wemding near Donauwörth, built in 1748–52 by F. J. Roth. In these his contributions as stuccoist and painter are once more important enough, as at Prien and Dietramzell, to enrich very positively the architectural effect of the interiors.

For the modelling in the late 1740s of St-Blasius, the Dominican church at Landshut, Zimmermann's fresco is dated 1749; as for Dietramzell earlier in the decade, no architect's name is recorded. But at the Benedictine abbey of Andechs above the Ammersee [Plates 48–50] he is known to have worked with Lorenz Säppel (1705–59) and the latter's advisor, the Prague-born Jesuit Brother Ignaz Merani (1693–1762) from Landsberg. In both cases, however, the homogeneity of the interiors suggests control by a single artist. At Landshut, where the thirteenth-century structural elements were considerably revised in the remodelling begun in 1747, if not at Andechs, which was re-modelled in 1751–5 under Abbot Bernhard Schütz for the 300th anniversary of the founding, one may well believe that Zimmermann might have had full responsibility. For such an attribution to Johann Baptist in the case of Andechs a project by him of 1751 for the east end [Plate 49], now lost, provides plausible if not quite clinching support (see pp. 33–5). With his brother also, at Steinhausen around 1730 [Plates 17–20] and at Die Wies [Plates 39–45, 56–8] in the late forties and early fifties, one may assume even without documentary evidence that there was a real collaboration of equals: the painter-stuccoist most probably had something to say about the architecture – and almost certainly about the stucco-work – and the architect-stuccoist something about the general scheme, at least, of the great frescoes overhead that play so important a part in the spatial composition.

The essential stylistic unity of the whole range of the Zimmermanns' mature activity from the late 1720s to the mid-50s is underlined by the very satisfying way in which later accessories, if still Rococo, enhance the over-all richness even of those churches that were originally built relatively early in the period. At Steinhausen [Plate 17], begun in 1727, Joachim Früholzer's altars date from the forties, fifteen years after the church was physically complete, although they admittedly follow very closely Dominikus's original designs of around 1730. At Günzburg as at Steinhausen the altars are based on Dominikus's original designs, in this case of 1736, but they were not executed by Ignaz Hillebrand and Ulrich Stengle until twenty years later, in 1757–8 [Plates 31, 32 and 34].

The situation is likely to be different when it comes to churches dating from before the 1720s. Whether or not the interior of the Neustift outside Freising, which was built by the Italian–Swiss G. A. Viscardi (1645–1713) in 1710–15, was to any considerable extent modified architecturally by J. M. Fischer when he restored or rebuilt it after the fire of 1751, it was only partially translated from Baroque into Rococo by J. B. Zimmermann's stucco and fresco decoration of 1756 and by the contemporary altars of Ignaz Günther (1725–75). After a fire of 1744, however, the Baroque reconstruction of the Gothic rotunda at Ettal near Oberammergau carried out in 1710–26 by another Italian–Swiss, Enrico Zuccalli (c. 1641–1724), was very much more effectively transmuted into Rococo by Joseph Schmuzer, assisted in the stucco decoration by his son-in-law J. G. Übelherr (1700–63), who had earlier been an assistant of J. B. Zimmermann's, under a fresco filling the whole dome painted by J. J. Zeiller (1708–83) in 1751–2.

In the secular field the Great Hall at Nymphenburg [Plate 53] was rather less completely transformed by François Cuvilliés (1695–1768) and J. B. Zimmermann, then seventy-six, in 1756–7 for the Elector Max III Joseph. The earlier Corinthian order of pilasters was retained, though the academic entablature was cut through by the arches of the Music Gallery, above to the west, and lightly decorated elsewhere with motifs in stucco in the advanced *rocaille* version of the Rococo that had first come into Germany some fifteen or twenty years before. It is, however, the bolder *rocaille* enframements of the frescoes on the walls and the rich vignetting of the ceiling fresco that dominate this gorgeous late interior. The stucco-work in the subsidiary Garden Room and Music Gallery, executed presumably from Cuvilliés's designs and therefore somewhat more delicate, is also appropriately devoid of the gilding so profusely employed in the Great Hall. (The gilder Lauro Bigarello actually received almost twice as much as Johann Baptist for his work.) Although at this late date they were certainly largely executed by Johann Baptist's son Franz Michael Zimmermann (1709–84), the stucchi in the Great Hall are among the most masterly the father ever designed, and quite different in character from the relatively restrained decoration that the two had just completed at Schäftlarn, on the Isar a little above Munich, presumably for J. M. Fischer (see p. 81) [Plates 51 and 52].

But drastic remodelling and redecoration of existing interiors is more characteristic of churches than of palaces. Dominikus's first really considerable work, in 1711–12, was the provision of stucco-work on the vaults and new scagliola side altars in the modest medieval church of the Carthusian monastery at Buxheim [Plate 2] where he had a year or two earlier undertaken several minor decorative commissions. One of the latest of his brother's was for the much more drastic renovation of the large medieval abbey and pilgrimage church of the Benedictines at Andechs. The former was hardly very successful, although the narrow nave and the sixteenth-century gallery cutting off the choir made the job peculiarly difficult, and funds were evidently very limited. But surprisingly enough Andechs, like Ettal, came out as one of the most exemplary Rococo interiors, thanks more (one may assume) to Johann Baptist than to Säppel, who was nominally in charge, or his not inexperienced adviser Merani, who was responsible in these same years for the design of the large, handsome new Jesuit church of Heilig-Kreuz above Landsberg.

Johann Baptist's project of 1751 for the high altar and the east end of Andechs already shows some of the essentials of the rather unusual scheme carried out over the next four years [Plate 49]. The most conspicuous features are the elaborate two-storey altar, a feature lately most notably used by Dominikus in the choir of Die Wies but here already present in simpler form since 1607–9, and the shallow gallery that passes in front of the upper altar and winds its wavy way round the walls of the whole interior [Plates 48, 50]. Thus the considerable height of the medieval hall-church was visually split in two, though the four westernmost of its six original tall slim piers were retained to carry the vaulting of the unified squarish space of nave-plus-choir. Connections with Dominikus's galleried choirs at Günzburg and Die Wies suggest themselves, as also with several of the new monastery libraries, especially that by Thumb at Sankt Peter, begun in the mid-thirties, which was just being completed and decorated at this time.

But even more striking are the curious near-parabolic shapes that resulted from filling in the heads of the pointed Gothic arches with flattened curves, a device not unknown in other such remodellings of Gothic churches though rarely so happily employed as here. The longitudinal arches, moreover, spring in a quite late-medieval way directly from pilaster strips without capitals at a level corresponding to the top of the architraves of the entablature-blocks on the sides above whose cornices rise the higher transverse arches. The slight horizontal emphasis of these blocks is, moreover, effectively counteracted by the upward scrolling of their cornices, a treatment not uncommon since the proto-Rococo work of the Asams in the early twenties. Thus the normal Renaissance relationship between supports and arches, very generally retained elsewhere even in this period by such leading architects as J. M. Fischer and Neumann, is quite avoided by the idiosyncratic detailing here of their juncture.

In this wholly exceptional vessel, still structurally Gothic, Johann Baptist then covered all the curved surfaces overhead with large ceiling frescoes set within richly scallopped frames of stucco, opening up the vaults illusionistically. Additional stucco decoration, in this case at least and often elsewhere, quite masks the real shape of the underlying severies of the Gothic vaulting, the original ribs being either removed or plastered over. There is nothing of the Baroque tradition left here except for the actual frescoes and the special sort of elaboration of the various altars. One must, therefore, consider this to be essentially a new work of Rococo interior architecture, not merely a Gothic church that has been 'baroquized' by profuse Rococo decoration, whether the responsible designer was Zimmermann, Säppel, or Merani. But Andechs was only one of the latest in a series of successful Rococo transformations of large medieval churches in southern Germany.

New altars, pulpits, and other large and elaborate pieces of church furniture such as organ-cases were frequently introduced both into medieval churches and into churches of the seventeenth and early eighteenth centuries. This was, of course, true of several of the scagliola altars designed and executed by Dominikus Zimmermann before his career as architect really began. Thoroughgoing redecoration of earlier Baroque churches, however, comparable to such major examples of the eighteenth-century remodelling of medieval churches as Freising Cathedral and Andechs, is not so common. Such work, moreover, is mostly late – of the 1750s – and usually not in very large or important churches. Three with which the names of one or other of the Zimmermanns are associated with more or less certainty deserve brief mention in this connection: Weyarn, Raitenhaslach and Gutenzell.

Weyarn, on the autobahn south-east of Munich, has an Augustinian abbey church built by the Swiss-born Lorenzo Sciascia (1643–94) in 1687–93. The interior of this derives almost all its artistic interest from the rich investiture of stucco-work and frescoes that J. B. Zimmermann provided in 1729 – early German Rococo of a very superior order, yet rather different from his ceiling in the Benediktbeuern library of 1725 [Plate 10] – and the superb sculptures by Ignaz Günther (1725–75) that were added in 1763–4 [Plate 21]. Johann Baptist's supposed association in the late thirties with Raitenhaslach, where the church had been rebuilt within Romanesque walls after 1694, is rather doubtful since the fine stucco-work is more firmly documented to Michael Zick, otherwise rather obscure. The extensive frescoes of 1738–9 are definitely not by Zimmermann but by Michael's better-known father Johann Zick (1702–59), who later painted the ceiling of Neumann's Garden Room in the Würzburg Residenz before Tiepolo came to work there.

At the Cistercian nunnery of Gutenzell near Biberach, founded in the fourteenth century, where the church had been built in 1518 and then 'restored' or, in fact, largely rebuilt after the Thirty Years' War in 1647, the interest of the eighteenth-century redecoration is partly associational. Above the high altar, dated 1763, appear the Zimmermann arms. This is because Dominikus's daughter Maria Alexandra, long a nun there, had become abbess in 1759. In 1755–6 Dominikus was paid 53 gulden 30 kreutzer for a 'Riss' or design. (The gulden or florin was, as its alternative name perhaps implies, more or less equivalent in value to an eighteenth-century English florin, i.e. two shillings.) But another man, probably the master-mason Nikolaus Rueff, later received 1,199 gulden for carrying out the work. The stucco decoration was commissioned at 1,300 gulden from 'H(err) Feucht Mayor Stockador von Augsburg' – presumably F. X. I. Feuchtmayr, since his son-in-law Rauch is mentioned as the assistant – and the contract with J. G. Dieffenbrunner (1718–86) for the frescoes, five of Old Testament subjects in large oval frames on the vaults and twelve of the Apostles on the side walls of the nave, was at 1,500 gulden. These figures do not suggest that Dominikus's responsibility for the work was very considerable.

This modest interior [Plate 55], with its nearly flat saucer vaults and its nave arcade inherited from the seventeenth century, is not one of Dominikus's more important works, if indeed his design was actually followed when the remodelling was carried out. It is, nonetheless, a characteristic example of rather late Rococo redecoration and an interesting contrast to the small churches with which his architectural career began a generation earlier [Plates 2, 3, 5, 11, 12]. But the credit must go largely to Feuchtmayr and Dieffenbrunner, neither of whom ever worked with Dominikus elsewhere.

Gutenzell, at least, is more attractive than another very late work that is definitely by Dominikus, the modest village church at Eresing, north-west of the Ammersee, that he remodelled in 1756–7. There, however, since the fifteenth-century structure was unvaulted, he retained the completely flat ceiling, handling it somewhat like those in St-Kassian at Regensburg (as remodelled in 1749–60) or at Arlesheim in Switzerland (as redecorated in 1759–60), the one almost certainly, the other most probably without benefit of architect. The stucco-work, rather richer than Feuchtmayr's at Gutenzell, was carried out here from Dominikus's designs by Nikolaus Schütz (†1785) around a large ceiling fresco, dated 1757, by F. M. Kuen (1719–71), both of whom had worked for or with him at Steinhausen. Thus Dominikus ended his career collaborating still with long-familiar associates, though not with his brother Johann Baptist.

*　　　*　　　*

Having dealt briefly and out of sequence with the very latest professional activity of Dominikus, contemporaneous with the ending of Johann Baptist's career by death in 1758, it is time to turn back to the Zimmermanns' beginnings. Artistically and professionally, they both matured rather late, in the 1720s, when they were well into their forties. Of apprentice-work preceding Johann Baptist's earliest recorded employment in the Benedictine monastery at Tegernsee in or soon after 1706 and Dominikus's scagliola altars of 1708 at Fischingen, nothing is known.

They were born – Johann Baptist in 1680, Dominikus in 1685 – at Wessobrunn-Gaispoint near Weilheim. After the death of their father, Elias Zimmermann (1656–95), a modest stone-mason and stucco-worker, their mother, born Justina Rohrmoser, remarried another stucco-worker, Christoph Schäffler, in 1696. The young Zimmermanns had their first artistic contacts, therefore, in the mid and late 1690s, respectively, with the local school of stuccoists, famous since the sixteenth century, of which both their father and their stepfather were undistinguished representatives. Dominikus is believed by some scholars to have been for a year or two an apprentice under Johann Schmuzer (1642–1701), father of Joseph Schmuzer, then the leading Wessobrunn stuccoist and architect. He was only sixteen when the elder Schmuzer died, but this training would probably have begun when he was fourteen. Since he is known to have married Therese Zöpf, of another Wessobrunn family of stuccoists – his own godfather was Thomas Zöpf – at Füssen in 1708, some have further guessed that he was then working under J. J. Herkomer (born c. 1650) who had begun in 1701 the church of St-Mang there. But by 1708 Dominikus was already being employed in his own right in Switzerland, at the Benedictine abbey of Fischingen in Canton Thurgau, to execute the scagliola altars in the Iddakapelle, begun in 1704 by Brother Christian Huber. His name, moreover, does not appear among the stucco-workers who assisted Herkomer.

Johann Baptist had married in 1706, two years before his brother, and may possibly have settled in Miesbach that year after a probable period of study in Augsburg concerning which no documentary evidence survives. More certainly this was when he first worked at the Tegernsee monastery. In 1710 he became a citizen of Freising and lived there for some years, being employed to decorate the cloister of Freising Cathedral in 1716.

The earliest known joint commissions of the Zimmermanns were for decoration of the sacristy, the library and the church of the Carthusian monastery at Buxheim just west of Memmingen, in 1710–12 [Plate 2] when Johann Baptist was already thirty and his brother twenty-five. (The redecoration of the Marienkapelle at Buxheim was initiated a year earlier, apparently by Dominikus alone.) Johann Baptist was busy also in 1710 with the decoration of the large new church of the Edelstetten Frauenstift [Plate 1], designed the year before by Father Vogt and carried out by Simpert Krämer (1679–1753), and in the sacristy of the Augustinian abbey church at Waldsee. Thus their effective beginnings coincide closely in date with the early patronage of the French Rococo by Germans in France (see p. 39) and precede by some years the introduction of the Rococo into Germany by the French- and Paris-trained foreign and German artists first employed in 1716–17 by the Wittelsbach Elector Joseph Clemens of Cologne and his brother, the Elector Max Emanuel of Bavaria (see pp. 39–40).

As late Baroque stuccoists Johann Baptist, and to a lesser degree Dominikus, became in this decade increasingly competent craftsmen abreast of Bavarian, if not yet of international, stylistic developments. (Finer and more advanced work was already being done in Franconia, however, in Schloss Weissenstein at Pommersfelden for Lothar Franz von Schönborn and in the Cistercian monastery at Ebrach nearby by Daniel Schenk [†1737], who is believed to have come from Breslau, and Georg Hennicke [†1739].) The Zimmermanns were starting also, without much training so far as is known, to practise as painter and as architect, respectively, rather than merely as stuccoists. If, indeed, Dominikus had worked in his youth under Johann Schmuzer and later under Herkomer, he would already have had considerable contact with the building profession in all its branches; certainly his altars from the first made much use of the orders and other conventional elements of Baroque architectural design. As has already been noted, Johann Baptist had been working in fresco from 1710, if not earlier, and may have studied in Augsburg before that.

From 1720 on the elder Zimmermann, then forty, came to play an important part in the Bavarian court circle of architects and decorators; his younger brother did not then, or indeed ever, work for the successive Bavarian electors. Yet one must suppose, even though Dominikus had settled in 1716 some distance away from Munich at Landsberg, that he was familiar by the mid-twenties with the interiors on whose decoration his brother had for some years been collaborating at Schleissheim [Plates 8 and 9] not to speak of Johann Baptist's library ceiling at Benediktbeuern of 1725 [Plate 10]. By then the Rococo was, of course, well established as the dominant mode of design in France and had been for some fifteen years. To those earlier years it will be well to turn at least briefly.

The Rococo had its beginnings – its actual genesis, according to the plausible thesis of Fiske Kimball – in work carried out for Louis XIV in the royal châteaux, especially the Ménagerie and the Grand Trianon at Versailles and at nearby Marly. For these interiors many new chimney-pieces and some complete sets of panelling were designed in the office of Jules Hardouin Mansart (1668–1708), the *premier architecte du roi*, around 1700 by Pierre Lepautre (*c.* 1648–1716), who had been taken on as a *dessinateur* in the Mansart office in 1699. By 1710 – the date is Kimball's – a German princess, Elisabeth Charlotte, usually known as Liselotte, daughter of the Wittelsbach Elector Palatine Carl Ludwig and widow of the duc d'Orléans, Philippe (I), was employing Germain Boffrand (1667–1754) to decorate various rooms in the Hôtel du Petit Luxembourg in Paris in the still very new Rococo style.

During the War of the Spanish Succession, in which they were both lined up on the French side, the Elector of Bavaria and his brother the Elector of Cologne were in exile in France. The elder, Max Emanuel, had already employed Boffrand before the (for him) disastrous Battle of Blenheim in 1704, to begin Bouche-fort, a hunting lodge outside Brussels, where he had earlier lived while Stadholder of the Austrian Netherlands. In 1713 he employed Josef Effner (1687–1745) to remodel, with Boffrand's advice, a house at St Cloud near Paris that is no longer extant. A son of the gardener at the electoral Schloss in Dachau, Effner had been called to Paris in 1706 by the elector to study garden design, but had soon joined Boffrand's circle. All through the long years of exile Joseph Clemens was in correspondence with Robert de Cotte (1656–1735), Mansart's brother-in-law and successor, concerning work to be done at his principal seat in Bonn; and in 1714 Max Emanuel obtained from de Cotte plans for the new Schloss at Schleissheim, the construction of which had been in abeyance for ten years while Austrian and allied troops occupied Bavaria.

It was the return of the two electors to their German territories after the Treaty of Rastatt brought the War of the Spanish Succession to an end in 1714 that occasioned the introduction of the French Rococo into Bavaria and the Rhineland. Max Emanuel brought Effner back with him and was soon importing other Paris-trained artists to work with him in Bavaria, and Joseph Clemens obtained designs from de Cotte and even from G. M. Oppenord (1672–1742).

De Cotte's rather timid Early Rococo projects for interiors in the Buen Retiro wing at Bonn of 1716–17 and Oppenord's for one chimney-piece can be ignored here, but not the Pagoden-burg in the gardens of Nymphenburg. This was designed in 1716 by Effner, who had been appointed *Hofbauintendant* the previous year, though Zuccalli retained until his death in 1724 the superior rank of *Oberhofbaumeister* or *premier architecte* of the electoral court. The Early Rococo rooms here, in a garden pavilion that echoed on a smaller scale the cruciform plan of Boffrand's Bouchefort, were variously decorated with Dutch blue-and-white tiles, with lacquer panels of Japanese design, and with carved wood panelling (*boiserie*). The stucco- and plaster-work inside and out by the Antwerp-born but Paris-trained Willem de Groff (*c.* 1680–1742), the ceiling paintings by the Austrian J. A. Gumpp (1654–1719), who had earlier frescoed the walls of Viscardi's Bürgersaal in Munich, and above all the *boiseries* by the probably Tyrolean-born but certainly Paris-trained J. A. Pichler (†1761?) reflect with real success the early French Rococo of Pierre Lepautre, though the tiling still recalls Louis XIV's first Trianon de porcelaine. The decoration of the Pagodenburg was completed in 1719.

The next work undertaken at Nymphenburg, the Badenburg pavilion of 1718–20, on the other side of the extensive gardens that the imported French designer Dominique Girard (†1738) was laying out, has far less connection with the Rococo. Perhaps this is because Effner had just returned from a belated Italian tour, while the Frenchman who executed the stucco-work, Charles Dubut (1687–1742), was Italian-trained and had not come directly from Paris but from Berlin. There he had worked under the Baroque sculptor and architect Andreas Schlüter until the latter's death in 1714. The frescoed ceiling in the principal interior is by the Italian Amigoni (1675–1752).

The centre of electoral building activity now moved to Schleissheim where J. B. Zimmermann came on the scene. Since he was brought there in August 1720 as a stuccoist, it was no impression that might have been made by his still rather limited accomplishment as a fresco-painter, but that of his stucco decorations of 1714–19 at Ottobeuren [Plate 4], a monastery often visited by Max Emanuel, or those of 1716 in the cloister at Freising Cathedral that led to his call to join Effner's team.

There are various different kinds of relevant interest in what was carried out at Schleissheim under Effner's direction in the last seven years of Max Emanuel's life. As evidence of the enthusiastic acceptance at the electoral court by this time of the Rococo as an almost unadulterated import from France, the Long Gallery on the garden front and the gold-and-white and silver-and-white *boiseries* in the suites of apartments for the Elector and the Electress to the south and to the north are certainly very notable. There was nothing else so advanced stylistically in Germany or Austria at this time even in Schenk's stucco-work of the previous decade at Pommersfelden or Roth's at Ellingen of 1718–20 for the Deutsch Orden, of which the grand-master was then the Wittelsbach Elector of Trier, Franz Ludwig von der Pfalz-Neuburg.

In these Schleissheim rooms the *boiseries* by Pichler, whether restricted to chimney-breasts or extending over most of the walls, are much in advance of his modest work in the Pagodenburg and even of what he had executed since in the Nymphenburg Schloss. Especially significant is J. B. Zimmermann's ceiling, probably of 1724 or 25, in the smaller chapel (Kammerkapelle) at the end of the Electress's suite. Pichler was not employed there, however, for the walls are of seventeenth-century scagliola intarsia brought from the Munich Residenz and installed and extended by J. G. Baader, who had worked earlier in the Badenburg at Nymphenburg. Except in the Kammerkapelle and the Electress's Writing Room, which is quite similar, Johann Baptist probably had little part in this portion of the work at Schleissheim. There is no more stucco-work in most of the two suites of apartments than in the Pagodenburg; indeed, many of the ceilings are painted quite in the Italian way. The *stucchi* of these years on the walls of certain ground-storey rooms have, however, been not implausibly attributed to him, despite the fact that the associated fresco panels are by Cosmas Damian Asam, who worked more usually with his brother Egid Quiriu as collaborating stuccator.

Johann Baptist's participation a year or two earlier in the decoration of the larger public rooms of the Schloss seems to have been more considerable though it is difficult to determine the sequence of execution and how much, if any, of this work is his own design. Dubut would certainly have had more of a say than the younger German, while both worked under the direction of Effner as architect. The Stairhall, the Great Hall, and the Hall of Victories are upstairs on the entrance front of Zuccalli's central block of 1701–4. Rising a full two storeys, so that they receive light not only from the front but also from over the Long Gallery at the rear, their noble size and shape, so completely Italianate, so alien to the French Rococo scale of the rooms behind, is certainly due to Zuccalli. Italianate also are the ceiling frescoes, that by Amigoni in the Great Hall filling the entire space from cornice to cornice, and the earlier and smaller one by C. D. Asam over the Stairhall. The latter is on the vaulted surface of a round lantern above a lower opening, somewhat as in his church at Weltenburg, where the ceiling fresco, dating from 1721, is almost precisely contemporary, or in the Stairhall of Hildebrandt's Palais Daun-Kinsky of 1713–16 in Vienna.

The treatment of the walls of these great rooms merits more

detailed description. In the Hall of Victories, decorated in 1724–5, the gold-and-white *boiserie* panels by Pichler, still wholly in the French Rococo mode of the previous decade like those of the large upper room in the Pagodenburg, contrast awkwardly with the great size and boldly plastic aspect of the stucco *atlantides* in the attic zone below the upper cornice they so sturdily support. (This very tectonic and Baroque treatment derives, curiously enough, from the de Cotte project of 1714.) However, in the coved and bracketted lower cornice of this room under the attic and in the framing of the over-mantel there would seem to have been a conscious attempt on the part of Effner and Pichler to increase the scale of these typically Early Rococo features to roughly twice that of the decoration on the *boiserie* panels. This introduced a third element, one that already offers premonitions of a specifically German Rococo interior architecture. But the result is rather incoherent, since the decoration of the room was carried out by several different hands and not fully controlled by Effner as architect in charge, or so it would appear.

Far more unified in design, if less advanced stylistically, is the Great Hall [Plate 8]. Except for the big battle paintings at either end by F. J. Beich (1665–1748), which date from 1702–4, the walls are entirely decorated in white stucco of *c.* 1723–5 with no *boiseries*. Most of that decoration must have been executed, though not designed, by J. B. Zimmermann. The general effect, despite the considerably greater size and height of the room, is less conservative than that of the hall of the Badenburg where Amigoni had painted the ceiling and Dubut executed the stucco-work a few years earlier. The inspiration is still predominantly Italian, however. On the other hand, the absence of an entablature above the giant pilasters – or even of entablature blocks – with Amigoni's fresco framed only by a rather heavy reeded roll-moulding, and especially the fashion in which the C-scroll decoration at the top of the curious curved members that take the place of entablature blocks curls up over the roll-moulding, with tendril-like extremities overlapping the edge of the fresco, suggest analogies with the then current handling of cove-cornices in France quite as much as does the lower cornice in the Hall of Victories, which is probably very little later. Yet the particular reason for this treatment here may well have been the very high placement of Zuccalli's upper range of arched windows rather than any desire to echo Parisian domestic interiors.

In the detailing of the stucco the delicate grillwork under the scrolled pediments above every other opening in the lower range and the naturalistic floral elements, behind the putti over the intervening openings, have a slightly French air. But comparison with Zimmermann's truly Rococo ceiling of a year or so later in the elegant little Kammerkapelle [Plate 9] seems to indicate either that he had as yet little knowledge of Rococo ornament when he was working in the Great Hall or that his associates there, Effner and Dubut, left him little freedom. Both are probably true. Grill work is much more profuse in the Kammerkapelle and the putti are much smaller. It would be very interesting, moreover, to know who – Effner or Zimmermann – was responsible for the design of the lantern over the chapel. Totally devoid of the conventional columnar elements used earlier in the lantern above the Stairhall, this represents a very early manifestation, if a modest one, of purely Rococo three-dimensional invention, such as would soon be much exploited in Germany for altars, and organ-cases in churches, and later in porcelain. For all the virtuosity of the Kammerkapelle ceiling and the fascinating evidence it offers of Zimmermann's early mastery of the imported Rococo, the Great Hall, considered as a whole, is more important historically – even though it is only the urns centred between the putti over alternate openings there, prefiguring those which provide the corner motifs in the Kammerkapelle and often appear in his later work, that seem already to carry Zimmermann's signature.

If one compares the Great Hall, for example, with that masterpiece of the French Régence, the Galerie dorée in the Hôtel de Toulouse in Paris, of which the redecoration was completed in 1719, the year before the major campaign of decoration at Schleissheim got under way, one may well be struck with similarities as well as with differences; nor do all the differences mark the French interior as the more advanced. The sculptor–decorator F. A. Vassé (1681–1736), whom Kimball supposes to have been more directly responsible than the nominal architect de Cotte, continued to use a full entablature above the pilasters, even though their shafts are not fluted, but panelled in the new Rococo way. Conversely, the podia below the pilasters are as plastically curved at Schleissheim as in Paris, although the curve is inverted. The membering above the doorway at one end of the Galerie dorée and the big mirror over the chimney-piece at the other, in both cases breaking up through the main entablature, is somewhat simpler and much flatter than that over the lower openings at Schleissheim; yet the sculpture on top of these features is bolder in scale. Above all, the retention of the compartmented framing of the existing paintings on the vault in the Hôtel de Toulouse, following the tradition of Le Brun's in the Galerie des glaces at Versailles, was still conservative in contrast to Amigoni's vast and unified fresco.

The Galerie dorée is generally recognized as the largest and richest Rococo interior surviving from the years when Liselotte's son Philippe II, duc d'Orléans, ruled France as Regent. It is, moreover, quite exceptionally monumental in scale, though lacking the double height of the nearly contemporary Galerie d'Oppenord of 1719–20 in the Regent's own Palais Royal. Effner's Great Hall, on the contrary, must still be considered generically Late Baroque. It is the difference between the rounded ends and the curved corners, respectively, of the galleries in the Palais Royal and the Hôtel de Toulouse and the plain rectangular plan of the Great Hall at Schleissheim [Plate 8], inherited from Zuccalli, that has the greatest stylistic significance at this point. Even so, the crowning elements over the awkward half-pilasters in the corners at Schleissheim are so set diagonally that they provide, above cornice level, a slight softening of the rectangle, somewhat as do the diagonally placed urns on the coved ceiling of the Kammerkapelle above the square-cornered scagliola entablature. In this respect, at least, the quadrantal corners that Effner had provided in the Badenburg hall of 1718–20 were more premonitory of planning developments in the mature German Rococo period. But a relevant forward step in this regard had been taken even earlier in the nave of St-Egidius in Nürnberg, rebuilt by Gottlieb Trost (1672–1728) in 1711–18, and before that in the small village church at Kreuzpullach, south of Munich, erected by some unidentified architect in 1710.

Except for his ceilings in the Kammerkapelle and the Writing Room, J. B. Zimmermann can not be allotted much personal credit for the design of the stucco-work at Schleissheim, though he seems to have gone on working there down to Max Emanuel's death in 1726. But his next commission was wholly his own. At the Benedictine Abbey of Benediktbeuern the library occupies a free-standing rectangular building erected in 1722–4 by the local builder Josef Hainz (†1763), probably from a design supplied by the monastery's cabinet-maker Ötschmann, as has been noted earlier. The library, now used as a refectory by the Salesian Brothers who run a school in the former monastery, is a large plain room of modest height, rather more generous in its vertical dimension than Dominikus's library at Buxheim of fifteen years earlier but without the surrounding gallery – or, today, even the bookcases – of the Ottobeuren library of 1715–18 [Plate 4].

It was doubtless as much on the recommendation of the Benedictines of Ottobeuren as on Johann Baptist's reputation as a member of the electoral team of craftsmen that Abbot Magnus Pachinger called on him in 1725 to decorate the low and largely flat ceiling here with stucco-work and frescoes [Plate 10]. Most of the frescoes, as in Zimmermann's earlier work from Edelstetten onwards, occupy rather small fields, here set along the centre line of the ceiling and at the cardinal points. Large ceiling frescoes were still rarely executed in south Germany except by Italians or artists who had been trained, like Rottmayr and C. D. Asam, in Italy. Urns full of flowers, with putti round them bearing scientific instruments and, in the centre, coats-of-arms occupy the smaller panels. There are also two larger panels whose diagonal compositions owe a good deal, presumably via Amigoni, to seventeenth-century Venice. These present the Benedictine Order as Supporter of Ancient Learning and an elaborate Allegory of the Sciences.

Except in the central armorial panel the perspective is not aerial as in Amigoni's and C. D. Asam's ceiling frescoes at Schleissheim. The compositions can therefore be appreciated only by placing oneself below in the proper position for each. But in the small panels at the cardinal points there is a most ingenious illusion: curved balustrades in stucco, recalling the painted balustrades Asam used at the edge of his epoch-making ceiling fresco of 1720 in the nave at Aldersbach, over which moulded and coloured drapery falls, seem to support the painted urns and also to define the space in which the painted putti disport themselves. Such balustrades were to be a recurrent theme wherever Johann Baptist was asked to combine his frescoes with stucco-work, even when the stucco-work was designed by his brother. Another favourite theme of Johann Baptist's stucco decoration, probably no more religious in its symbolism here than in the Schatzkammer of the Munich Residenz six or seven years later [Plate 22], is the fountain, rising from a flower-like cup, that is repeated here on the diagonal in all four corners somewhat like the urns in the Schleissheim Kammerkapelle [Plate 9].

The rather consistently Rococo character of this ceiling, no surprise after that of the Kammerkapelle – if, indeed, it follows rather than precedes that – depends partly on the considerable use of specifically Early Rococo elements of band-work, foliated C-scrolls, areas of grillwork, and the similar reticulated patterns the French rather confusingly call *mosaïque*, not to speak of delicate floral garlands, and semi-naturalistic tendrils. But it depends, still more significantly perhaps, upon the near-arabesque effect resulting from the even deployment of the motifs – though only the frames of the panels above the balustrades consist literally of arabesque elements – and the very slight projection of the cream-coloured decorative elements from the flat white plane in relation to the large area of the whole ceiling. The few figures executed in stucco are in lower relief than the putti of the Kammerkapelle, as are also such other sculptural features as the naturalistic birds and the grotesque masques. The scallopped framing of the two large frescoes, however, is still rather heavy and solid. This is to be interpreted less, perhaps, as a continuation of Baroque practice than as an augury of the degree to which Rococo scale in Germany would soon be increased from the domestic intimacy, so truly French, of the Kammerkapelle ceiling to the monumentality of the great church interiors that the Zimmermanns and others would shortly be executing, a development already initiated in the Asams' redecoration of Freising Cathedral in 1723–4 just before this.

Dominikus's two well-preserved churches of these years, that of the Dominican nunnery at Siessen, for which his contract is dated 1725, and the parish church at Buxheim, are both rather small. An earlier church incorporated in the Dominican monastery in Schwäbisch-Gmünd, completed by others long after Dominikus's brief building campaign of 1724–5, was too drastically damaged when the monastery became a barracks in the nineteenth century to be worth discussing. There is also his church for the Ursuline (now Dominican) nuns at Landsberg from these same years of the mid-twenties. There the elaborate scheme of frescoed decorations of 1765 by J. G. Bergmüller and other later emendations are more conspicuous than Zimmermann's original conception of the interior. However, the galleries at the west end, one above another, are quite like those at Mödingen.

Siessen, where the circular frescoes, in the three bays of the nave, in the crossing and in the choir are by Johann Baptist, is hardly of the quality of the Benediktbeuern library, if that be considered not in terms of its neutral architecture but of its inventive decoration. The confectionery colouring of the stuccowork at Siessen, as refreshed in the post-war restoration, suggests 1872, the date of the earlier renovation when the high altar of 1762–3 was so unfortunately removed, rather than the eighteenth century, and certainly contrasts most unhappily with the pure cream-and-white of the Benediktbeuern ceiling. Equally deplorable are the present gaudy tonalities and unpleasant textures of the heavily restored frescoes. In the decoration at Buxheim, however, probably slightly later than Siessen, at least as regards the stucco-work surrounding the frescoes – dated 1727 and not by Johann Baptist but by F. G. Hermann (1692–1769) – how much Dominikus was learning of the new Rococo style in the mid-twenties, presumably from his brother, is much more agreeably evident [Plate 12]. As both Siessen and Buxheim must have been designed not more than two years before Dominikus's first architectural master-work, the pilgrimage church at Steinhausen, and had not received their stucco-work and frescoes before that was begun — one of Johann Baptist's frescoes at Siessen carries the date 1729 and the church was consecrated only in 1733, the same year as Steinhausen — it will be better to proceed now to a description of the latter without commenting further on these minor works.

Rarely has the work of an architect risen so suddenly from mediocrity to mastery, and for this no explanation seems adequate. It is even a little surprising that the Dominican Prioress Josefa Baizin, the client for Siessen, should have recommended Dominikus so successfully to the Premonstratensian Abbot Didacus Ströbele of Schussenried for the much more important commission to build the great shrine at Steinhausen in 1727 when her own church, though the contract is dated 1725, was apparently only begun the previous year. What the Siessen church cost is not known, but Dominikus was eventually paid the fee of 4,000 gulden mentioned in the 1725 contract in 1728 and Johann Baptist received 100 gulden each for his five frescoes. Construction of the large quadrangular nunnery over the years 1716–22 for Prioress Baizin from the designs of Franz II Beer (1660–1726) had required only 24,333 gulden, 16 kreutzer; but the church probably cost considerably more than that, as one may judge from what was paid the Zimmermanns. Doubtless Dominikus had originally much underestimated the cost when called on to design the church the year before Beer's death. However that may be, his first optimistic estimate of 1727 for Steinhausen (which would eventually cost 48,495) was only 9,000 gulden!

That improbably modest figure must have appealed to Ströbele when he called on Zimmermann to build the new pilgrimage church. Neither he nor Dominikus could have foreseen in 1727 that by the summers of 1730 and 1731 over 200 craftsmen and ordinary workers would be employed, much less that all the altars in their final form and other fittings would not be in place before 1749–50. This was to be long after proceedings had been taken against Ströbele at the time of the consecration (1733) for diminution of the monastery's funds thanks to the already excessive sums spent on the church. (The prosecution led to his banishment to a monastery in Alsace, which explains why it is not Ströbele's arms but those of his successor as Abbot of Schussenried, Siard Frick, that appear above the main portal.)

Despite his very low initial estimate, Dominikus must have intended from the first that Steinhausen should be of an order of architectural magnitude for which none of his previous or current church commissions had prepared him. It is not that Steinhausen is so very much larger than his earlier churches — the nave of Mödingen is 20·85 × 13·3 m, that of Buxheim

18 × 11 m, and that of Steinhausen, without the aisles of
1·8 m, only 25·5 × 14·5 m – nor that it is free-standing where
all the others, even the Buxheim parish church, are attached to
conventual buildings; it is rather that the entire architectural
conception is more original, indeed effectively unique, and the
decoration more integral than in any of his work or that of
his contemporaries except the Asams' decorations in Fischer's
church at Osterhofen, dating also from the late twenties and
early thirties.

Mödingen, Siessen and Buxheim, as presumably also Schwäbisch-Gmünd and certainly the Landsberg Ursulinerkirche, have
conventional rectangular naves without aisles but with fairly
deep narrow choirs ending usually in rounded apses. Thus the
two spatial elements are visually discrete and, in fact, often seem
quite awkwardly adjusted to one another at the chancel arch.
The only spatial variation Dominikus had introduced hitherto
was the very slight transeptal projection at Siessen, more conspicuous externally than internally because of its scallopped
gables. Steinhausen, however, is in plan an oval surrounded by
piers carrying elliptical arches that intersect the base of the oval
dome [Plate 15]. The shallow choir is a harmoniously related
smaller oval set crosswise. This is approached through an axial
eastern arch which is, like that at the other end, wider and more
flattened than those at the sides of the nave. Externally the oval
plan is largely disguised by gabled rectangular projections to east
and west, and also along the middle of the sides, so that the curved
shape of the interior is suggested only in the segmental quadrants
at the corners [Plate 16].

Oval church plans were no novelty. They had been a consti-
tuent part of the Italian tradition since Vignola's Sant' Anna dei
Palafrenieri in Rome, designed in 1572. Indeed, the shape had
been continuously popular with architects active in Rome, from
Francesco da Volterra's San Giacomo degli Incurabili, finished by
Maderno at the opening of the seventeenth century, to Rain-
aldi's Santa Maria dei Miracoli, completed in 1679, and especially
so with the two greatest High Baroque architects, Bernini and
Borromini. The Asam's Weltenburg, begun in 1716, is a sort of
Berninian oval. Moreover, the leading Austrian architects of the
previous generation, J. B. Fischer von Erlach (1656–1723) and
Hildebrandt, had been building oval churches in Salzburg and
Vienna since before the opening of the century – Fischer's Dreifaltigkeitskirche in Salzburg dates from 1694 and his prominent
Karlskirche in Vienna, begun in 1716, was approaching completion
at this very point. Since intimate or even first-hand knowledge
of these Austrian churches on Zimmermann's part is unlikely,
it is probably more relevant that J. M. Fischer was beginning in

this year (1727) the Hieronymite church of St-Anna-am-Lehel
in Munich, of which the plan is a somewhat Guarinian variant
of the simple oval, though deriving more probably from Christoph
Dientzenhofer's Obořište in Bohemia, begun in 1702, than
directly from a Piedmontese model.

Although the proportions were later made longer and
narrower [Plate 15], the Steinhausen nave from the first [Plate
13] was intended to be ringed by single piers and provided with
a narrow aisle cut off where it was overlapped by the smaller
oval of the choir. If the special characteristics of the Steinhausen
arcaded oval – the single, free-standing supports and the axial
location of the central one on either side – are considered
significant, as distinguished from the coupled supports and
transeptal cross-axis of Zimmermann's later church at Die Wies
[Plate 40], it can be said that there exists for Steinhausen no
executed prototype; nor is there really even any closely similar
project, so far as is now known, by an Italian or a German architect
from the century and a half since Vignola's aisle-less oval church
was designed. For Die Wies, curiously enough, the later Zimmermann church, the *atrio* of Guarini's Palazzo Carignano of 1680 in
Turin can be cited – despite its secular purpose and its transverse
axis – as a model possibly known to Dominikus by repute or
from the engravings that were published in 1686. Among many
oval church projects with coupled supports as at Die Wies,
moreover, one may note as probably the earliest of consequence
Mascherino's for Santo Spirito dei Napolitani in Rome of the late
sixteenth century, preserved at the Accademia di San Luca, and
among later examples several by Caspar Moosbrugger (1656–
1723) for the choir of Einsiedeln in Switzerland. Some of the
latter, if hardly Mascherino's, might have been known to
Zimmermann. There were also oval projects prepared early in
the 1720s by de Cotte, by Boffrand, and by Maximilian von
Welsch (1671–1745) for the chapel in the Würzburg Residenz,
some of which Dominikus might have seen when he was
working in the Neumünster at Würzburg in those years.

For one important particularity of Steinhausen the cited
Italian and German examples, executed and unexecuted,
provide little precedent – the use of square piers faced with
pilasters instead of round columns [Plate 17]. But such piers are
common in south German churches while columns, freestanding
or engaged, were not so often used.

If the interior of Steinhausen were divested of all its stucco
decoration on pilaster capitals, on entablature blocks, and in the
pendentive zone of the vault, as well as of Johann Baptist's great
fresco overhead, one would have a simple domical canopy
carried on plain square piers inside the solid oval of the exterior

walls. To some extent doubtless this effect, perceived as it must be *through* the decoration that Dominikus so profusely provided, is evident to analytical observers. But to aesthetically innocent observers, such as the pilgrims for whom the church was built, the initial and dominant effect is quite different. Above the sturdy, solidly material piers that surround the worshipper at his own level the oval cylinder of the interior seems to open up to the skies where the Virgin as Queen of Heaven soars in glory [Plate 19].

Seated on top of the entablature blocks the stucco figures of Dominikus's Apostles, some looking down, some looking up, call attention to the heavenly scene. Above them, at the base of the fresco, painted groups of figures representing the Four Continents occupy the diagonal positions. To the west, over an inscription giving the date 1731 and Dominikus's signature, Eve tempts Adam in a garden setting; while to the east, over the choir arch, the Fountain of Life in another garden setting rises above the inscription: HORTUS ES DEI GENETRIX FONS SIGNATUS.

The transition from the everyday world in which the worshipper stands or kneels to the world of heavenly illusion is a gradual one, each stage meaningful in itself yet also leading on, in terms of the relation between reality and illusion, to the next. In the three eastern and three western bays at the ends of the nave the pendentive zone surrounding the base of the dome appears relatively solid. The scrolled mouldings at the top are not unlike the broken pediments over the lower openings in the Great Hall at Schleissheim but are here bent inward by the concave surface of the dome. This concavity the illusionism of the fresco behind and above ignores, or rather, quite disguises. Over the paired bays in the middle of the sides the pendentive zone is crowned with urn-capped balustrades in relief like those at Benediktbeuern [Plate 10] through which the lower edges of the fresco are visible. On either side of these features white stucco putti tumble about swinging floral garlands in the real space of the observer. Their whiteness creates a further degree of abstraction beyond that of the polychromed Apostles; yet, thanks to their evident solidity, they are closer to human reality than the allegorical painted figures representing the Continents above and behind them.

But again those figures, which are not heavenly but of this earth, still have like the Garden of Eden to the west and the other garden to the east considerable reality of their own, since they are not very far above the observers' line of sight and stand on painted ground of rock or turf. Then, overhead in the high heavens, the Virgin, her angel attendants, and even the once-human saints are seen floating or perching upon clouds, their absolute size much diminished by illusionistic distance. In between, the open zone of frescoed sky symbolizes effectively the gulf between earth and heaven, between Time and Eternity.

The description in the previous paragraphs is very selective, omitting many points of intrinsic interest. As regards the plan and section of the nave, one should further note that the aisle is little more than a passage cut through deep radial wall-pillars that support the vault, much as in the vast Swabian abbey church at Weingarten, which had been completed a few years before, and other wall-pillar churches. There is a related statical explanation for the radial barrel-vaults over the aisle. They also provide buttressing for the dome while the little arches behind the piers actually serve as internal flying buttresses.

Johann Baptist's stucco-framed frescoes on the aisle vaults offer scenes from the life of the Virgin. What he painted on the oval dome of the choir is appropriately related more closely in subject matter to the miracle-working carved *Vesperbild* (Pietà) of *c.* 1415 on the high altar that had long been the *raison d'être* of the Steinhausen pilgrimage. There, surrounded by angels, God the Father and the Holy Ghost appear, ready to receive the Risen Christ. He is represented both by a floating stucco figure above the altar and again in a small oil-painting. This last, and the larger altar-painting of the Deposition below, which provides a most suitable background for the *Vesperbild*, are both by F. M. Kuen. These are both presumably of the same late date as the altar itself in its final form, that is 1749–50.

But enough of iconography for the present (see pp. 75–7). The principal *forte* of Dominikus's mature talent as architect– stuccoist – ARCHIT E STUCKADOR, as he signed himself here – was the construction of decoration. He was already here at Steinhausen, as he would be again at Die Wies, the anti-Pugin, the anti-Laugier, to name two later theorists who especially condemned the construction of decoration; no less, of course, are his ideals the antithesis of those of twentieth-century 'Functionalists'. The significant sources for Steinhausen must be sought along that line. As in the case of the plan, Zimmermann's own earlier churches offer little or no preparation for his achievement here. In designing and decorating them the architect seems to have set out with no coherent or total visual concept in mind. Moreover, whether the fresco-painter was Johann Baptist, as at Mödingen and Siessen, or another, as at the Buxheim parish church, there was no such happy collaboration as between the brothers here. One must look elsewhere for the steps that led to the notable triumph of the brothers at Steinhausen.

In the case of an architect such as Dominikus, who as far as is known never travelled abroad or even worked with any foreign-trained artist except possibly Herkomer in his early youth, local German sources must have provided most of his inspiration. Tracing the origin of vault-filling frescoes back, via Austria, to Italy, or of specific decorative motifs to France is rather unprofitable. Knowledge of seventeenth-century Italy and of the eighteenth-century Rococo of France could come to Dominikus only from engravings or, in his case far more probably, through his compatriots at second or, more usually, third hand. Yet such knowledge he had surely obtained by this time from his more experienced and sophisticated brother who was, in these years of the late 1720s and early 30s, still working in Munich in closest *rapport* with the cosmopolitan artists of the electoral court as he had earlier done at Schleissheim (pp. 57–8).

Perhaps significantly, the closest executed prototype of the Steinhausen plan is a secular one, the *atrio* of the Palazzo Carignano in Turin. In 1692, moreover, Viscardi had proposed something similar for Schleissheim. A German secular interior with which J. B. Zimmermann was actually associated, Effner's Great Hall of 1723–4 at Schleissheim, seems to have suggested some, at least, of the motifs in the constructed decoration at Steinhausen [Plate 19]. There, also, a vaulted ceiling is filled from rim to rim with Amigoni's illusionistic fresco, although that is bounded above a cove by a firm roll-moulding rather than vignetted by atectonic stucco-work [Plate 8].

At Metten on the Danube near Deggendorf, however, the nave of the drastically remodelled fifteenth-century Benedictine abbey church offers the closest prototype for the treatment of the pendentive zone at Steinhausen, as also for vignetting a fresco that all but completely fills the ceiling of a vaulted nave. The remodelling of the church here began in 1712 with the choir; then, in 1720, the walls of the nave were moved outward so that the old external buttresses became internal wall-pillars, with tall rounded chapels between. The design was supposedly provided by the Straubing city-architect, Rusch, but executed under the direction of the local mastermason Benedikt Schöttl (1688–1742). The stucco-work was commissioned on 15 May 1722 from F. J. Holzinger (1691–1775), an Austrian from Schörfling on the Attersee, who was already responsible for the polychromed stucco decoration in the monastery's sumptuous library completed two years before.

The young C. D. Asam had already provided the painting for the high altar, for which he was paid 1,500 gulden at the opening of his career in 1715, and later that for the altar of the Virgin. The frescoes on the ceiling and the north side of the choir are also attributed to him. Furthermore he is known to have prepared a sketch for the ceiling fresco in the nave. A drawing for a very large ceiling fresco of the Glorification of St Michael, evidently suitable only for a church dedicated to St Michael as is Metten, actually survives in the Staatliche Graphische Sammlung in Munich. But Abbot Roman Märkl evidently changed both the subject of the painting and the painter. The existing fresco of the meeting of Benedict and Totila was executed not by Asam but by Innozenz Waräthi (c. 1690–1758), like Holzinger an Austrian from Sterzing in the Tyrol. He began work in 1724 when the Asam brothers were both busy first at Freising Cathedral (1723–4) and then in the Benedictine abbey and pilgrimage church at Einsiedeln in Switzerland (1724–6), which may explain his employment in place of C. D. Asam.

There are many differences between the Metten ceiling and that at Steinhausen, however. The barrel-vaulted nave at Metten is necessarily rectangular in plan, though the actual field of Waräthi's fresco is very slightly ovalized by curves at the corners – as was already proposed by Asam in his extant sketch, if that be in fact for Metten. White stucco putti here and there overlap the fresco and at the front corners paint clouds overlap the stucco frame in the Bacciccian mode that was just then being boldly exploited for the first time in Bavaria by the Rome-trained C. D. Asam at Freising. The frame, however, even though scallopped in outline, consists of a continuous, rather stiff moulding that is barely broken above the transverse severies at the sides by tight cartouches with little or no Rococo character. Moreover, the stucco border is interrupted over and between the tops of the flanking severies by small fields of fresco alternately heart-shaped and roughly triangular.

Aside from the intrinsic superiority of J. B. Zimmermann's fresco to Waräthi's, with its brilliant fresh colouring, its lovely landscapes at the ends, and its persuasive aerial illusionism overhead, the close collaboration of the brothers at Steinhausen resulted in a much more masterly handling of the pendentive zone and a wholly different spatial effect [Plates 17–19]. Not surprisingly, considering Johann Baptist's precisely contemporary work for Cuvilliés in the Munich Residenz [Plate 22] the stucco-work, even though designed by Dominikus, incorporates many specifically Rococo elements and even approaches Rococo delicacy of scale. Yet, above all, it is the wonderfully even lighting of Steinhausen, strong but never glaring, which differentiates it from such a relatively dark earlier church as Metten. This lighting one finds again at Die Wies [Plates 42 and 43] and at Schäftlarn [Plates 51 and 52]. It is, indeed, characteristic of most mature German Rococo interiors.

The furnishing of Steinhausen with organ, altars, pulpit and confessionals took a long time [Plate 17], as has already been noted. Although Früholzer executed the present high altar only in 1749–50, he followed Dominikus's original design; and Dominikus, earlier a specialist at altar design himself, must certainly have envisaged from the first the effect of its focal presence and that of Früholzer's side altars of 1746, shining in black, grey and mottled reddish scagliola with white statuary and gilded accents, in contrast to the matt-white stucco of the piers. The rich dark tone of the high altar and the shallowness of the choir make the tiny early Pietà before Kuen's oil-painting of the Deposition very prominent, as is proper for the principal object of devotion in a pilgrimage church. On either flank of the choir arch the tall side altars, moreover, are not set back against the walls of the aisles but at the inner line of the piers of the arcade. Rather inconspicuous balconettes extend behind them one bay to the west, and also continue eastward along the curved sides of the choir to the high altar. These arrangements much increase the visual prominence of the side altars in the whole composition of the interior.

At the west end the concave-fronted organ-gallery projects into the central oval of the nave and also extends behind the piers on either side, thus balancing the balconettes behind the side altars [Plate 18]. Organ gallery, pulpit, and balconettes introduce, above all, a more human measure in contrast to the tall piers and the nearly 20m height of the oval dome at its crown. Unlike the big earlier nuns' galleries at the west end of Mödingen [Plate 5] and Siessen or the later one at Gutenzell [Plate 55], the raised elements here do not clutter or consume the main space of the nave; but they are not as elaborated plastically as by Dominikus at Günzburg and Die Wies in the 1730s and 40s or by Johann Baptist and his associates at Andechs in the 50s [Plates 32, 43 and 49].

The exterior of Steinhausen makes a very different impression from the interior [Plate 16]. The dominant rectangular elements at the ends and sides offer no promise of a unified oval interior. The tall and broken skyline, characterized by pointed roofs and by scallopped gables similar to those over the transeptal projections at Siessen, almost seems to imply a pre-Baroque date in the late sixteenth or early seventeenth century. The modest tower, with a bell- or helmet-shaped roof rather than the traditional 'onion' of the region, rises like an afterthought over the western projection. Only the treatment of the individual elements of the façades suggests the Early Rococo. The concave pilaster capitals, with their lambrequin-like appendages at the top of plain shafts, not an uncommon motif by the late 1720s, are elaborated from those on the otherwise very plain nunnery at Mödingen [Plate 6], begun after the church there in 1720 and only brought to

completion in these years. But the prominent window shapes —
not especially noticeable inside, since they are usually only
glimpsed between the tall piers of the nave arcade — are of a
fantasy peculiar to Dominikus Zimmermann.

Dominikus had already used windows with scallopped tops in
the projecting bays of the Mödingen nunnery. At Siessen and at
Buxheim [Plate 11], moreover, he had introduced above the
plain arched windows at the sides strange, somewhat Guarinian,
triplets with central rectangular lights bowed both at top and at
bottom and flanked by shorter ear-like side-pieces. Such windows
he repeated in the upper range here, following more closely the
Buxheim than the Siessen model, that is with the 'ears' right
side up instead of inverted. The taller windows below have
triconch arches at the top, as at Mödingen, but their jambs scroll
outward like question marks just below the arch. These curious
shapes were further embellished inside: garlands hang over
the ears in the upper range; delicate relief decoration fills
the intradoses of those below; and putti are even perched
upon a string-course that bows upward over the lower openings.

Dominikus's commissions were almost always ecclesiastical;
Johann Baptist, after his call to Schleissheim in 1720, was as
much or more concerned with work for the electoral court as for
the monasteries and nunneries that were his brother's usual
clients. Named *Hofstuccateur* in 1729, his secular work reached
its climax in the thirties. But before turning to that it may be
well, in relation to Steinhausen, to deal at least summarily with
the churches and monasteries he was also decorating in these
years from the late twenties to the mid-thirties.

In 1729, just before he started work with Dominikus at
Steinhausen, in decorating the Augustinian church at Weyarn
that the Italian-Swiss Lorenzo Sciascia (1643–94) had built in
1687–93, Johann Baptist showed again, as earlier in the Benediktbeuern library in 1725 and also in St Martin at Dietramzell in
1726, how much lighter was his hand as a stuccoist than his
brother's [Plate 21]. Identifiably French Rococo ornamental
elements are more frequent here than at Steinhausen. Only in the
two bays of the choir, however, are the frescoes, also by Johann
Baptist, actually vignetted by stucco-work, and even so this
follows the framing of the small scenes from the life of the
Virgin on the aisle vaults at Steinhausen more closely than
Dominikus's constructed decoration on the pendentive zone in
the nave there. Even lighter was his touch the following year in
the stucco decorations he provided for the Augustinians at nearby
Beyharting in a church that was medieval in origin, but had been
extensively remodelled in 1668–70 by Konstantin Bader. Thin
garlands and sinuous palm-branches are the principal features of

the decoration here rather than the more abstract elements of the Rococo decorative vocabulary; while the fresco panels, smaller relatively than at Weyarn, are quite rigidly framed, with no approach at all to vignetting.

Far more successful, however, is what he provided in 1731–2, just after Steinhausen, on the ceiling of the large but low hall (Neuer Festsaal) at Benediktbeuern [Plate 23], which had been built by Hainz, presumably to Ötschmann's designs, in 1728–31. This is, not surprisingly, well advanced beyond his library ceiling there [Plate 10] but is in worthy succession to it, as are also the more modest decorations in the corridor outside and the nearby Stairhall. Stucco-work on the jambs and soffits of the windows and doors, which have characteristically Rococo segmental heads, relieves the plainness of Hainz's architecture and the double cove of the ceiling makes up somewhat for the modest height of the walls. In contrast to the library, a rather large fresco occupies the centre of the ceiling and the floral and foliate elements of the surrounding stucco-work have a truly spontaneous air. Additional smaller frescoes occupy the ends and recur on the sides as well as along the cove. Their themes are familiar in palace decoration – the Four Seasons and the Four Elements – but the subject of the robing scene in the large central panel, though presumably related to the history of the Benedictine Order or of this abbey, is not readily identifiable.

Compared to the elegance of this secular – or at least semi-secular – interior, now used by the Salesians as a school chapel, Johann Baptist's church decorations that follow in the mid-thirties are disappointing. One must, in fact, query his reputed responsibility for the stiff patterns of the stucco surviving on the choir vault in the Würzburg Neumünster – his frescoes on the nave vault were destroyed in the war. The frescoes and stucco-work he executed in 1734 in the church of the Cistercian nunnery of Seligenthal at Landshut which J. B. Gunetzrhainer began in 1732 deserve more attention however. Interesting, at least at this relatively late date, is the extreme delicacy of the stucco on the shallow vault of the nuns' gallery over the nave. Perhaps intentionally almost domestic, even feminine, rather than monumental in scale, this seems to provide a sort of transition between his work for Cuvilliés in this decade in the Munich Residenz [Plate 22] and the bolder treatment he used over the crossing, the transepts, and the choir here. In the crossing the stucco figures of the Church Fathers on the pendentives are in high relief, quite in the Italian way of Pietro da Cortona's in Santi Luca e Martina in Rome or C. D. Asam's *grisaille* frescoes at Weingarten of 1718–20; while the large fresco of the Coronation of the Virgin, occupying a circular frame like his frescoes at

Siessen and many others of this period by Asam and others, provides the partial illusion of a high dome.

More advanced towards the mature ecclesiastical version of the Rococo in Germany is the treatment of the choir ceiling. The frame of the rather small fresco there is an irregularly scallopped oval, such as the Asams had for the first time used in a large German church at Aldersbach in 1720, and the distribution of the stucco decoration on the vault surfaces is, as at Benediktbeuern, much more even. But the spatial organization of Gunetzrhainer's church, though aspiring to the grandeur of his contemporary Damenstiftskirche (St-Anna) in Munich, which the Asams were engaged in decorating at this very point, is somewhat incoherent thanks chiefly to the deep nuns' gallery covering the entire nave.

Of Zimmermann's contemporary stucco-work and fresco decorations in the Chorfrauenkirche at Nymphenburg, begun by Effner in 1730 and consecrated in 1739, nothing remains after the bombing of the 1940s. Despite bombing, which destroyed the splendid Grüne Galerie of 1733, there fortunately still exist many other well-preserved, or at least very skilfully restored, examples of Zimmermann's collaboration with Cuvilliés in the Munich Residenz and in the Amalienburg at Nymphenburg dating from the decade 1729–39.

Plans for extensive reconstruction of the Munich Residenz, especially the wings beside the sixteenth-century Grottenhof, were prepared by Effner in 1725, but the work had hardly begun when Max Emanuel died the following year. The project was continued by the next elector, Carl Albrecht, but almost all that had already been accomplished was shortly wiped out by a fire in December 1729. Of the new campaign of decoration in the Residenz that began in 1730 not Effner but Cuvilliés took charge. Cuvilliés had returned from four years of study under François II Blondel (1683–1748) in Paris in 1724 and the following year received an appointment as *Hofbaumeister* (court-architect) under Effner, who continued until the end of his life in the higher position of *Oberhofbaumeister* to which he had succeeded on Zuccalli's death. In that year 1724 Cuvilliés built in Munich the Palais Piosasque de Non, which was destroyed in the war, and in 1728 he was employed by Carl Albrecht's brother Clemens August at Brühl in succession to J. C. Schlaun (1695–1773). Not surprisingly Cuvilliés's work showed from the first a far more consistent mastery of current French practice than Effner's, being refined and often academic as regards exteriors and ebulliently Rococo in interiors. The façades of the new construction were completed by 1731 and also the rooms on the ground floor – the Ahnengalerie (Gallery of Ancestors) and the Schatzkammer (Treasure Room, now Porzellankabinett) – although it took until 1737 to bring the entire suite of electoral apartments above – now appropriately called the Reiche Zimmer – to completion.

The Ahnengalerie, remodelled by Effner from a garden room dating from 1580, survived the fire of 1729. Some at least of the stucco decoration on the vault by Zimmermann, above *boiseries* of 1729–30 by the Bohemian-born Wenzeslaus Miroffsky (†1759), is thought to date back to 1728–9 before Cuvilliés became the directing artistic figure at the Munich court. The bold scale of the cove cornice with its richly scrolled brackets, recalling Schleissheim, which doubtless inspired Zimmermann's smoother cove in the Benediktbeuern Festsaal [Plate 23] of 1731–2, and the sharply scallopped framing of the three inset oil paintings on the ceiling by B. A. Albrecht, so similar to that of Zimmermann's earlier ceiling panels of 1725 in the Benediktbeuern library [Plate 10], contrast with the French delicacy of the tendrils and the scroll-work round them. This contrast may well reflect the shift in architectural control at the Residenz from Effner to Cuvilliés after the fire, even though all the stucco decoration here was almost certainly executed by Zimmermann.

Since the *boiseries* by Joachim Dietrich (†1753) – like Miroffsky the product of Paris training – in the Schatzkammer (which was projected by Cuvilliés in 1731) are dated 1733, one may perhaps assume that the superb stucco ceiling there by Zimmermann [Plate 22] is a year or two later than the richer but less original one in the State Bedroom in the upper storey, the first of the Reiche Zimmer to be carried out from Cuvilliés's designs, with *boiseries* of 1732 by Miroffsky. But whatever the precise sequence of these and other ceilings by J. B. Zimmermann in the Reiche Zimmer, all later than that of the Ahnengalerie below, they are closer in spite of their luxuriance to the finest French plasterwork of the period than to his brother's bolder and more original stucco decoration at Steinhausen [Plates 17 and 19], which must be of almost precisely the same years as the earliest of these, or even, for that matter, to his own more restrained work of these years at Weyarn, Beyharting, and Benediktbeuern [Plates 21 and 23].

For posterity, if not necessarily for contemporaries, the Munich rooms are overshadowed by the still greater luxuriance and the climactic quality of the Amalienburg interiors of 1734–9 at Nymphenburg outside the city. Concurrently with their work for him in the later Munich Residenz, Cuvilliés was also employing at the Amalienburg J. B. Zimmermann, Dietrich – though no longer Miroffsky – and probably also the Antwerp-born but Paris-trained sculptor Egÿd I Verhelst (1686–1749). (Zimmermann, as has been noted earlier, may also have been working still for Effner at Nymphenburg in the Chorfrauenkirche attached to the Schloss.)

Under Max Emanuel some sort of a pavilion associated with pheasant-shooting, located in the gardens of the Schloss to the south of the main axis, balanced his hermitage-like retreat, the rustic and pseudo-ruinous Magdalenenklause with its chapel, which was begun by Effner for the elderly Elector, grown belatedly pious, in 1725 and consecrated by Clemens August for his brother Carl Albrecht in 1728. In 1734 Carl Albrecht ordered the construction of a new '*Lusthaus, genannt Amalienburg* [for his wife Maria Amalia] *und einen neuen Fasanen gartten nebst einem Bruedhaus*'. Despite the kennel-room, with its painted vignettes in blue on white by the Munich-born but Paris-trained Pasqualin Moretti (*c.* 1700–58), and the recurrent hunting motifs in all the decoration, the twentieth-century visitor is unlikely to find the extreme luxury of these interiors any more suitable for a hunting lodge than most Protestants feel Rococo decoration to be for churches. (Except for the relatively late Ludwigskirche in Saarbrücken by F. J. Stengel [1694–1787], built 1761–75, Protestants even in Germany generally eschewed Rococo, and even advanced Baroque forms, for their churches.)

The central Spiegelsaal (Mirror Room) has some claim to be considered the most beautiful of all eighteenth-century interiors [Plates 25 and 26]. Even before its completion, moreover, Cuvilliés's first book of designs, the *Livre des cartouches* of 1738, had so successfully made his personal Rococo style available as a model for international emulation that he was encouraged to follow it up within a few years by the even more influential *Livre de lambris* and *Morceaux de fantaisie* (both undated). In 1745 a new edition of the first work appeared. There can be little question that here, as fifteen years earlier for Effner at Schleissheim and just before this for Cuvilliés at the Residenz, Zimmermann was an executant carrying out with virtuosity the designs of another artist, in this case a decorative designer of the highest individual talent, not to say genius. Although there is some stucco-work by Zimmermann on the exterior of the Amalienburg – Diana the Huntress accompanied by putti and symbols of the chase over the main entrance, and hunting trophies between the flanking pilasters – discussion must be confined here to the great circular room in the centre, even disregarding the superb Bedroom and Hunt Room that flank it to north and south.

The evident resemblance of the Spiegelsaal to the Salons ovales carried out by Boffrand in the Hôtel de Soubise in Paris, built originally by P. A. Delamair (1676–1745), especially to the Salon de la princesse, and the early employment of Boffrand by Carl Albrecht's father, not to speak of Effner's certain and

Cuvilliés's presumptive connexion with Boffrand during their earlier years in Paris, have led many writers to imply that in the Amalienburg the Paris rooms were directly imitated. Fiske Kimball wrote, for example, in a note in *Le Style Louis XV*, 1949: '*Le pavillon d'Amalienburg . . . , bâti par Cuvilliés dans le courant de 1734 où la décoration du Salon est très évidemment basée sur celle du Salon de la princesse, était achevé en 1739. . . .*' Yet in his text he said of the Parisian rooms that '*le travail semblerait avoir été commencé en 1735 ou 1736*', citing a statement of Delamair (who should have known since he had been the original architect), and went on to state that the paintings in the Salon de la princesse were completed in 1739 or 40. In the captions of Kimball's illustration, moreover, the Salon du prince is dated '*vers 1737*' and the Salon de la princesse, flatly, '1738–40'(!) The interior elevations of these rooms were published by Boffrand only in the forties.

This does not, of course, exclude the possibility that fairly detailed projects for the Salons ovales existed on paper by 1734 of which Cuvilliés might have seen copies. But it does make it extremely unlikely if not, indeed, impossible that the Amalienburg Spiegelsaal derives from the *executed* rooms in Paris. Allowing for Cuvilliés's Paris training, yet recognizing from the great originality of Steinhausen the evident possibility of autochthonous architectural creativity in southern Germany in these decades, a creativity increasingly independent of either Italian or French models, it may be well to consider how closely in fact Cuvilliés's salon does resemble Boffrand's (as Feulner did so ably forty years ago in his *Bayerisches Rokoko* even without having very exact knowledge of the dating of the rooms in Paris).

In the first place Cuvilliés's room is circular not oval. This is rather surprising considering the popularity of oval plans in eighteenth-century Germany – the most comparable secular interior in Bavaria of earlier date than this would be the Oval Saloon in the Schloss at Alteglofsheim near Regensburg (whose architect is unknown) with frescoed ceiling of 1730 by C. D. Asam. Next, one may note that in the salons in the Hôtel de Soubise the conventional Rococo panels of *boiseries* are carried only to impost height between the arched niches in which the doors and windows are set, while only three in the upper salon, and none in the lower, are filled with mirror. At the Amalienburg niches and more freely arched wall-elements of nearly identical height alternate all the way round. Except for the four doors at the cardinal points and the two windows flanking the entrance, moreover, all the niches as well as the spaces between are filled with mirrored panels. Such a profusion of mirror was long out of date in France. Considered together with the more even rhythm of articulation, this is certainly very different from the limited and syncopated use of mirror in Boffrand's rooms in Paris.

Above the arches in what may be called, as at Steinhausen, the pendentive zone, there are notable differences also: instead of the framed spandrel panels over the *boiseries* in Paris, filled with sculptured reliefs in the lower salon and with inset oil paintings in the upper one, at the Amalienburg a broad flat band, broken only by the cartouches above the niches, runs round beneath a coved cornice that moves freely both upward and downward. Moreover, that member itself is wider and bolder than the comparable element in Paris. Above the cornice-line the ceiling of the lower salon in Paris is quite flat and decorated only with a central ornament; the upper salon has radial open-work bands linking the central medallion on the very slightly concave surface with the cove at its edge. At the Amalienburg, however, the ceiling is much more domical. Moreover, the putti and other figures that perch on the cove-cornice, somewhat as in the Salon de la princesse, are provided with rocky seats and backed by naturalistic trees rising, rather like those in the landscapes at the two ends of Zimmermann's Steinhausen fresco [Plates 17 and 19], against the plain plaster of the vault which tells as an illusionistic sky. Today, this 'sky', like the rest of the background in the Spiegelsaal, is light blue, which helps to support the illusion; originally it was a sort of milk-white with only the faintest bluish tinge, close to the tone of the walls in J. B. Neumann's Weisser Saal of the mid-forties in the Würzburg Residenz, the most completely Rococo of all his works.

Not least of the differences is the use of silver in the Amalienburg, as earlier in the electress's apartments at Schleissheim, for all the relief elements of the *boiseries* and the stucco decoration, not only in the Spiegelsaal but in the rooms to left and right. For them, however, the background colours, now a rather strong egg-yoke yellow, were originally described as 'straw' and 'lemon'. The lower salon in Paris, on the other hand, is all white and the upper one, white and gold – as are most of Cuvilliés's earlier interiors at Brühl and in the Munich Residenz [Plate 22] – with colour only in the spandrel paintings of the Salon de la princesse.

How much independence should one assume that Zimmermann had in executing the Amalienburg stucco-work? One notes urns that recall his work at Schleissheim, Benediktbeuern and Steinhausen, where he was not associated with Cuvilliés; there are also a few fountains, as at Benediktbeuern and in his Steinhausen fresco. More significant, perhaps, than these motifs is a distinctly greater boldness of relief than in the work he had carried out in Munich for Cuvilliés or that at Weyarn, Beyharting and Benediktbeuern which he had done on his own. Is this the result of his association with Dominikus and the latter's 'constructed decoration' at Steinhausen? If so, it is hardly so evident at Prien [Plates 27 and 28], where Johann Baptist worked in 1738 with an architect other than either his brother or Cuvilliés.

However that may be, in the more abstract elements of the decorative vocabulary employed in the Amalienburg there are features and qualities that must represent not Zimmermann's personal contribution but rather Cuvilliés's mature intention of proceeding, as in the earlier Reiche Zimmer, well beyond what he had known in the Paris of ten years earlier. Notably, there is the ambiguity of the principal mouldings on the walls: these follow first the curve of the extrados of the niches, then turn outward below the spandrel panels of *mosaïque* to become, not the jambs of the niches, but rather those of the mirrors between, and finally end at the bottom in S-curves that still more definitely confine the mirrors. These divagations are almost unthinkable in the orderly Rococo of the seventy-year-old Boffrand, advanced though that was by this time beyond the timid rectangularity of the *boiseries* he designed in 1724 for the Würzburg Residenz. One thinks rather of some of the plates in the *Livre d'ornements* published by J.-A. Meissonier (1693–1750) in 1734, the model in many respects for Cuvilliés's own publications of 1738 and later, which must have become available almost at once in Munich; or, even more appropriately, of certain innovations by Nicolas Pineau (1684–1754), such as can be seen, for example, in the galerie of the Hôtel de Villars in Paris, dated 1733 by Kimball, which Cuvilliés might have known from drawings. Pineau had introduced his striking novelties in France only after his return from Russia, where he had worked for the Czar, just as Cuvilliés's boldness was undoubtedly encouraged by a client who was not French.

While Johann Baptist, in the early thirties, was becoming in the Munich Residenz the indispensable collaborator of another architect, Dominikus, who was still occupied with the completion of Steinhausen and even possibly Siessen, continued his career well away from the electoral court. In December 1732, he offered Abbot Rupert Ness several projects for the new church of the Ottobeuren Abbey where Johann Baptist had worked so long before. None of them was accepted and construction, on a plan of 1736 by Simpert Krämer, began only in 1737. (The church as we know it, however, was largely executed by J. M. Fischer, who took charge in 1748.) For this big abbey church, which would have been a commission of the greatest importance to him, Dominikus did not develop the ideas of Steinhausen in the way he would in the next decade at Die Wies. On the contrary one rather grand scheme [Plate 24], with a square nave and a square choir to west and east of a very wide central domed area, and fronted by a concave façade between two towers, might more readily be attributed, were it not signed, to Fischer, whose late church at Rott-am-Inn of 1759–63 it seems in plan to foreshadow. At the least, this project belies the usual picture of Dominikus as merely a very talented Bavarian peasant, for it illustrates a sophisticated awareness of various Late Baroque ideas of planning and massing unrelated to the more personal and more definitely Rococo character of his two greatest churches. Another project is somewhat more Zimmermannian, yet rather muddled: in this a quadrilobed nave precedes a narrower square choir and a still narrower apsed sanctuary.

The following year, 1733, Dominikus was put on a retainer by the Buxheim Carthusians for whom he had begun to work more than twenty years earlier. They kept him busy at first only with various odd jobs in the cloisters and elsewhere; but this eventually led, towards the end of his term of service, to his designing in 1738 the Annakapelle, a minor gem – for it is jewellery-like in its miniscule richness–to which we will return shortly (see pp. 67–8).

In 1734 he was made a member of the town council of Landsberg. But more relevantly, in June of 1736, the council of the imperial town of Günzburg on the Danube called on him to rebuild their parish church which had burned in the spring of 1735. Towards the new construction the Prince-abbot of Kempten donated window-glass, the Abbot of Zwiefalten 29 gulden and, in 1739, the year before he died, the Emperor Karl VI 4,000 gulden. This church, largely completed with the execution of the frescoes, signed and dated 1741, by the minor painter Anton Endele (1700–61), is similar in size to Steinhausen: the aisle-less nave is almost identical in length and width but the galleried choir to the east is 16·5 m deep. For various reasons, not least the great inferiority of Endele's frescoes to J. B. Zimmermann's, Günzburg has never been considered of equal importance to Steinhausen and Die Wies in Dominikus's *œuvre*.

Where the plan of Steinhausen is a plain oval, with inner arcade of square piers supporting the dome [Plate 15], a plan to which Dominikus would return with some modifications later at Die Wies [Plate 40], the oval shape of the interior here – under a domed ceiling constructed of wood, not of masonry as at Steinhausen – is much complicated below by the treatment of the walls [Plate 29]. The curvature of the bold cornice at the corners, above deep diagonal niches that are occupied by side altars to the east and by gallery stairs to the west, defines an interior oval within the rectangular shell of the exterior walls [Plates 31 and 32]. However, as in the Asams' Weltenburg of

1716–18, a very notable oval church located somewhat farther down the Danube towards Regensburg, where at this late date the diagonal altars in the corner niches had just been installed, Dominikus's cornice does not continue unbroken all the way round. The 'barrel vault' of the choir's plastered ceiling intersects the surface of the oval 'dome' at the east end of the nave and a similar arch rises before the flat west wall over the organ at the other end. Moreover, the transeptal suggestion of the flat external projections [Plate 30], resembling those on the sides of Steinhausen [Plate 16], is echoed internally by equally high and even broader arches at the centres of the sides.

Additional complication is introduced, first by the bold entablature-blocks of the free-standing columns that flank the corner bays and, secondly, by the almost indefinable curvatures in plan of those portions of the entablature that are over the paired free-standing and engaged columns set at the sides of the transeptal bays. This marked irregularity, so different from the consistent and unified treatment of the nave arcade at Steinhausen, is distinctly confusing. Moreover, the contrast between the strongly tectonic treatment of the order – symbolic of structure, yet without real structural function – and the delicacy and relative flatness of the stucco decoration in the zone above, executed from Dominikus's designs in 1741–2 by Thomas Gering, a local Günzburg craftsman, is even more disturbing. In exaggeration, one may say that the walls with their bold columnar phrasing are still Baroque, while the ceiling represents a more advanced stage of the Rococo than the constructed decoration of the pendentive zone at Steinhausen.

As in his ambitious Ottobeuren projects of 1732, Dominikus seems to have sought here to rival contemporary, or slightly earlier, churches by other designers. Placing the oval thus within a rectangle recalls J. M. Fischer's St-Anna-am-Lehel in Munich, begun in 1727, as well as C. D. Asam's Weltenburg. Moreover, the complicated movement of the entablature at the side at least suggests some relation to the handling of the upper zone in E. Q. Asam's own church, St-Johann-Nepomuk in Munich, begun in 1733, even more than it does Weltenburg. The columns perhaps echo the many free-standing ones in Neumann's chapel in the Würzburg Residenz, which he had begun in 1732 under Hildebrandt's dominant influence and which was by this time structurally complete, or the conspicuous engaged ones at the crossing and east end of Fischer's great church at Diessen on the Ammersee, also structurally complete by 1735 though decorated only after that date.

Fortunately, however, the dichotomy between Baroque pseudo-structure and Rococo decoration at Günzburg, so common henceforth in other south German churches where architect and decorator were not – as effectively here – the same man, is not as great as this detailed analysis tends to suggest. The capitals and the decorative friezes of the entablature blocks have a distinctly Rococo delicacy and freedom of design; while the stucco-decoration on the ceiling, if flatter than that at Steinhausen, still has a quite un-French breadth of scale that is nonetheless hardly Baroque.

In describing the plan of Günzburg mention has already been made of the length of the choir, more than twice as deep as that of Steinhausen [Plate 29]. This is a most important feature of the church, premonitory of that at Die Wies [Plate 40]. The two-storeyed scheme, with solid walls below and open galleries above set behind paired square piers, leads to a double altar – executed only in 1757–8 by Ignaz Hillebrand from Zimmermann's original designs – that fills the apsidal end. This scheme derives presumably from Johann Schmuzer's choir at Vilgertshofen near Wessobrunn of 1686–92, which Dominikus certainly knew in his early youth, whether or not he worked under Schmuzer there. (On the vault there Johann Baptist had actually renewed the frescoes only two years before.) On the ceiling of the Günzburg choir the stucco decoration is even more delicately Rococo than in the nave, rivalling Johann Baptist's contemporary work at Prien [Plates 27 and 28]. Old photographs, taken before the restoration of 1951–2, reveal how much this had been damaged by the darker and heavier polychromy of the restoration of 1902. However, the dark oil paintings set into the ceiling, rather like Albrecht's in the Ahnengalerie, now appear somewhat too much as dark spots against the light tones, with touches of gold and green that are presumably what Zimmermann intended. The brighter colouring of the frescoes on the nave ceiling is more consonant with the lighter tonality.

At the west end the broad gallery for the use of the nuns in the contiguous Franciscan nunnery balances in its scallopped convexity the concavity of that end of the nave. This is a happy way of handling a subsidiary feature, usually required in churches built for the use of nuns, which elsewhere, at Mödingen [Plate 5] and Siessen, and more particularly at Seligenthal and Gutenzell [Plate 55], destroys the spatial unity of the interiors. The detailing of the parapets and screens offered Zimmermann an opportunity for a sort of cadenza of open-work Rococo ornament towards which his treatment of the west end of Mödingen had led the way [Plate 40].

Externally, the Günzburg church seems considerably less rural and anachronistic than Steinhausen [Plates 16 and 30]. The very shallow pilasters, with much simplified flat capitals, phrase more proportionately the south wall of the nave, which is about all that is visible other than the tower, except from a distance across the Danube. Concave chamfers at the corners and complicated curving surfaces, echoing the meander of the interior cornice at the edges of the transeptal projections, give considerable plastic interest of a sort perhaps to be considered as specifically Rococo; while the typical Zimmermannian windows – keyholes on either side, triplets in the centre, and irregular oculi above – are more comfortably accommodated in their respective wall-bays than at Steinhausen. The tower, also, with its plain square medieval shaft, though standing where it blocks a good view of the choir, is more architectural in scale, and also more subtle in the shaping of the upper stages, than that at Steinhausen. The strong red and yellow of the present – presumably not original – colouring is better suited, moreover, to an exterior than the tender green and pink pastel tones used in the 1931 restoration of the exterior of Steinhausen.

How much was lost at Günzburg because Johann Baptist was not employed for the frescoes is suggested by his work in the parish church at Prien, where his vast ceiling fresco of the Battle of Lepanto in the nave is signed and dated 1738 [Plates 27 and 28]. The local architect Johann Steinpeisz, who began the church in 1735, had partially ovalized the rectangular nave by rounding the corners as J. M. Fischer had done so effectively ten years before at Osterhofen, and J. G. Fischer was doing at this point in his church for the Franciscan nuns at Dillingen. Zimmermann played up to this by introducing rather large cartouche-framed frescoes of patron saints of the parish in the corners of the vault, even though the main fresco overhead has approximately straight sides and ends. His damasked-stucco draperies held by flying angels, behind and above the rather plain side altars that are set in the eastern quadrants, are as bold in their free-flowing forms as in their rich gold-fringed fields of deep blue. There is little other strong colour, the stucco decoration being mostly grey or gold against a white ground, but with a good deal of gold *mosaïque*.

Two modest chapels by Dominikus were under way well before Günzburg was completed. The larger – 15 × 10 m with three subsidiary elements to the east 3·8 m in diameter – at Schloss Pöring outside Landsberg is hardly worth mentioning, having never been adequately decorated and furnished despite its status as a modest pilgrimage church. The triconch plan of the east end here is of some positive interest, however, since it precedes by several years that which J. B. Neumann provided at Gaibach. Interesting also – though negatively, as a curiosity – is the totally incompetent painting on the ceiling dated 1739. This is by

Dominikus himself, his one signed fresco, and very likely his only serious essay at emulating his painter-brother.

The Annakapelle at Buxheim of 1738–40, at the north-west corner of the cloister of the Carthusian monastery, though considerably smaller, deserves more consideration. In plan this is a circle within a square with deep lobes at the corners and scagliola columns at the angles between carrying a continuous scallopped entablature. The light, here very strong, enters through side windows in the lobes, through oculi above the cornice, and through the sidelights of a little terminal lantern above the domical vault. Over the altar is a large oil painting by Johann Baptist of the Virgin with Sts Anna and Joachim in a richly curved gold frame set well forward from the rear wall of the tiny apse and supported by winged putti [Plate 35]. Above float putti without wings who pull back a brocaded blue stucco curtain with heavy gold fringe suspended from an open-work corona. This corona actually extends into the main space of the chapel, thereby completing the circle of the apse. Up through it there is a glimpse, over the inter-twined M and A that crown the altarpiece, of a Berninian vision emulating, at pathetically reduced scale, that of Christ and God the Father by E. Q. Asam at Rohr executed nearly twenty years before. The figure of the Infant Christ is here silhouetted against a gilded glory and white clouds that are brilliantly lighted by the invisible oculi. Below the flying putti, at either side, statues of the two Sts John, standing in niches, call attention to the altarpiece. As pendants to these, additional statues of Sts Joseph and Judas Thaddeus, attributed like the two Sts John to Anton Sturm (1690–1757), occupy the niches in the other two corners.

All of this may be thought to belong to the international Late, not to say High, Baroque tradition. But the treatment of the vault surface above the entablature is more characteristic of Dominikus's maturity, since it incorporates as at Günzburg various specifically Rococo details [Plate 36]. Immediately above the cornice there is a zone of constructed decoration in white stucco analogous to that at Steinhausen. This is crowned with strongly plastic scrolled and broken pedimental elements, much as in the earlier church, on which are seated stucco statues, presumably by Sturm, of Sts Barbara, Katherine, Agatha and Ursula. On smaller reversed versions of similar S-curved elements above the entrance and the high altar putti are perched. Behind and above the bigger figures large plastic C-scrolls curve upward to form a pattern of reversed scallops round the base of the lantern. To this winged putti are precariously attached by stucco clouds overlapping the bottom of the lantern. Gilded floral garlands loop between the upper ends of the C-scrolls and the thighs or hands of the putti. Against a pale blue background white elements in relief, mostly taken now from the Rococo vocabulary of ornament, provide a lacy overlay very much more delicate in scale than the sculptural figures.

The total effect is certainly over-rich; it is also rather incoherent, as the previous paragraph may well have suggested. Moreover, the putti – hardly to be attributed to Sturm but presumably Dominikus's own work – are somewhat crudely executed, if hardly as rustic as the figure-style of the lamentable Pöring fresco. The visitor's first *éblouissement* on entering this tiny chamber tends gradually to evaporate as he becomes adjusted to its doll's-house size and capable of analyzing clearly the disparate elements of which its ultimately indigestible elaboration is made up. The contrast in the quality of the stucco-work with that by Johann Baptist in the Amalienburg [Plates 25 and 26], which was being brought to completion in these years, or even at Prien [Plate 27], is notable; and there is none of the generosity of scale and little of the architectonic assurance of Steinhausen.

It will be well to move on to Die Wies, of which the construction began in 1746, with consecration almost a decade later in 1754, for this is the culminating masterpiece of the Zimmermanns' joint careers. For the moment their other work of the 1740s may be largely ignored. Dominikus's design of 1741 for the Johanniskirche at Landsberg was in any case not carried to completion until 1750–52 (see pp. 78–9); and that of 1748 for the nave of Schongau was considerably modified in execution in the early fifties, though the stucco-work in the choir may be by him. The project for the Premonstratensian abbey at Schussenried [Plate 46], also of 1748, was eventually carried out with much reduction by Jakob Emele in the 1750s and 60s. As built, the splendid library there has little in common with Die Wies, although Dominikus rather than Emele has often received credit for it.

Johann Baptist's frescoes and stucco decoration of 1743–5 in J. M. Fischer's church at Berg-am-Laim and those of 1744–5 at Dietramzell are not especially relevant to his work at Die Wies; while the earlier Franziskanerkirche by Fischer at Ingolstadt, where Johann Baptist painted the fresco (and possibly executed the stucco-work) in 1740, was destroyed in the last war. St-Blasius in Landshut, which he decorated with stucco and fresco in 1749, is rather disappointing even after its lately completed restoration and need not be described here.

In the year 1745 that saw the serious initiation of the project for building Die Wies Johann Baptist was already sixty-five and Dominikus sixty. That year the Elector Carl Albrecht – Karl

VII as Emperor – died, bringing the War of the Austrian Succession to an end with Bavarian acceptance of Maria Theresia and her husband Francis of Lorraine as Empress and Emperor. So it was Carl Albrecht's successor as Elector of Bavaria, Max III Joseph, who was invited by the Steingaden Abbot Marian II Mayr to lay the cornerstone of Die Wies on 10 July 1746. A native Landsberger, and hence in some sense a fellow-citizen of Dominikus, Mayr had just succeeded in March of that year Abbot Hyazinth Gassner who had already commissioned Zimmermann a year or more earlier. It was Mayr – with only some 8,000 gulden in hand at the start – who carried the great financial burden of bringing the church to completion at a total cost of 180,000 according to Norbert Lieb's estimate. (In 1803, when secularized, it was still valued at 170,000 gulden.) That the Steingaden monks had little money to spare for the Ingenried parish church in these years is hardly surprising (see p. 23).

In discussing Steinhausen it was natural to consider the exterior only incidentally, as was almost equally true of Günzburg. But Die Wies, like most of J. M. Fischer's famous churches of these years, not to speak of Peter Thumb's Birnau, begun in 1746, and Neumann's Vierzehnheiligen, designed in 1744, is impressive from the outside, especially from a distance. The long mass crowns a rising site in a wide opening in the forest with high wooded hills behind [Plate 41] – Die Wies, indeed, means 'The Meadow'. The composition is distinctly episodic, however. The bowed front, with its engaged columns and its high curved attic, would seem to have been influenced by Fischer's façades at Zwiefalten and Ottobeuren. Yet the entablature blocks are warped in plan like those on Dominikus's later altars and thus less conventionally Baroque than those over Fischer's columns. But the order here, all the same, is hardly to be considered Rococo since it is so boldly tectonic.

The west front can no longer be seen head-on because of the large trees that grow close by; seen obliquely, the contrast of its plastic membering with the smooth side walls of the church is distinctly awkward. The idiosyncratic detailing of the order of columns set forward of the front wall is barely noticeable. The characteristic Zimmermann windows on the other hand, sparsely spotted on the convex sides of the nave but crushed together on the flat walls of the long choir, are conspicuous enough. These features are hardly more coherently organized by pilaster strips and decorative borders than at Steinhausen, while their location is so entirely determined by the interior arrangements that they seem from the outside to have been distributed almost without regard for composition. The slim tower beyond the choir, moreover, simpler than those at Steinhausen and Günzburg [Plate 30], is hardly an adequate vertical accent to the great length of the side elevations of the church and provides only a feeble link with the squarish blocks of the clergy house and the abbot's summer residence that bring the elongated mass to an end at the rear.

Once again, one is forced to realize that Zimmermann's interest – and hence his positive innovating talent – focused almost entirely on interior architecture. For all his attempts at lightening the scale and enlivening the exterior by twisting the entablature blocks of the columns and decorating the yellow side walls with painted white borders of vaguely Rococo character – more conspicuous since their late renewal – the massive two-pitched roofs of the nave and of the residential wings at the rear have a plasticity and a solid weight as Baroque as the swelling west front; that, indeed, is their major visual asset.

Something has been said earlier about possible sources for the plan of Die Wies (p. 49). It is now worth noting certain changes in Dominikus's intentions between his first ideas of the mid-1740s and the executed church. In an early plan prepared for Abbot Gassner [Plate 39], long preserved in the Episcopal Archive at Augsburg but destroyed in the last war, the piers were shown as quite thick in section and plastically elaborated by half columns towards the nave and on the sides. A shallow gallery, scalloped back from the piers, was to extend all the way round over the aisles as they do along the sides of so many churches of the rectangular wall-pillar type. In this early scheme the piers flanking the cross-axis, which is otherwise unaccented, are indicated as double, while those that flank the entrance and the choir-arch are single. Moreover, the nave is near to a true ellipse in shape – at least with no straight sections – even though the oval is a broad one, rather like that of Bernini's Piazza S. Pietro in Rome (which is, of course, geometrically not an ellipse at all).

In the executed church the nave is narrower, though not as narrow as at Steinhausen, and all the piers are double. The cross-axial middle bays on either side, moreover, as at Günzburg, are as wide as those to east and west, and the side walls are flattened both outside, as already at Steinhausen [Plate 15], and also inside as at Günzburg [Plate 29]. The slighter section of the piers was made possible by substituting, as at Günzburg, a high-coved wooden ceiling with a wide flat centre for a dome of masonry, like that at Steinhausen [Plate 14], such as was presumably intended in the early project. Moreover, the galleries were entirely omitted in each of the three side bays to the north and to the south. As at Günzburg [Plate 31], however, galleries flank the deep choir. These lead from the pulpit and the abbot's loge in the nave to the upper level of the double high altar. But, unlike Günzburg, there are groups of irregularly arched openings rather than solid walls at the sides of the choir below and single columns above rather than coupled piers [Plate 45]. The unusual size of the choir, completed and dedicated in 1749, five years before the church as a whole was furnished and consecrated, resulted from Abbot Mayr's fear, recorded in December 1745, that the Wies pilgrimage might not so prosper as to justify a very big church, in which case the choir alone could serve. But such deep two-storeyed choirs had long been known in south German pilgrimage churches: the late seventeenth-century one at Vilgertshofen has been mentioned, and that probably derives from an earlier seventeenth-century example at Polling.

Features initiated or developed at Günzburg certainly play an important part here, yet over-all the resemblance to Steinhausen is closer. It is proper, therefore, to compare this late masterpiece of the Zimmermanns more particularly with their early one of twenty years before.

As is especially apparent from outside, Die Wies is much larger than Steinhausen although the internal height of the nave – 20 m compared to 19·5 m at Steinhausen – is almost the same. But the length of Die Wies is 59·4 m and that of Steinhausen only 44·4 m. The nave is 17·5 m wide, moreover, with aisles of 2 m, where the Steinhausen nave is 14·5 m, with aisles of 1·8 m. There are three rather more important differences, however: the provision of the deep, galleried choir for the reasons noted; the coupling of the supports round the nave as in most of the possible prototypes for these two churches that were mentioned earlier (see pp. 48–9); and the considerable emphasis on the cross-axis.

Despite the flat external projections at the sides, the nave arcade at Steinhausen describes a true ellipse internally. Here at Die Wies, however, the sides of the nave arcade are so much flattened that the shape is, if not the by-now fairly common south German one of a rectangular nave somewhat ovalized by rounded corners, at least that of an oval distorted towards the rectangular by straightening the sides. The result, therefore, is quite similar to the shape of such an important Early Rococo secular interior as the Galerie d'Oppenord of 1717 at the Palais Royal in Paris, not to speak of the Festsaal of the abbey of Metten, begun in 1734 presumably by Benedikt Schöttl, and J. G. Fischer's churches of the 1730s at Wolfegg and Dillingen, which may well have been known to Dominikus. Indeed, looking up at the scallopped cornice at the top of the pendentive zone, one can see that the near-oval is also slightly squared off at the east and west ends. The actual shape of the ceiling fresco within its frothy vignette of stucco is, therefore, like Johann Baptist's at Prien [Plate 27] and many of the other large frescoes that all but completely cover the ceilings of rectangular naves since Waräthi's of the 1720s at Metten, rather a scallopped rectangle than a scallopped oval. In fact, the stucco crestings at the centres of the sides, as also the illusionistic steps rising to the frescoed Throne of Judgement and Gate of Eternity at the ends, actually seem to bow inwards instead of following the concave curve of the oval.

These are somewhat subtle points, more evident to analytical twentieth-century scholars such as Wolfgang Lotz than to eighteenth-century or later pilgrims. But what everyone must notice, in contrast to Steinhausen, where the sides of the nave curve continuously and piers are set on the cross-axis, is that here at Die Wies there are openings at the centres of the sides of the nave arcade as wide as those to east and west – 7 m, in distinction to the diagonal bays of 4 m – and that behind these openings there are large altars set against the flat outer walls, altars that are much more approachable than the great two-storeyed one at the far end of the choir [Plate 52].

The supports in the nave of Die Wies are not merely coupled rather than single as at Steinhausen, they have a quite different cross-section. Instead of the square Steinhausen piers with their applied pilasters, these approximate circular columns; yet they have sharp corner arrises projecting between their rounded sides. Thus they actually resemble the sort of Late Gothic pillars described as 'prismatic', even though they are not set diagonally. Some earlier eighteenth-century architect, perhaps Viscardi's successor, J. G. Ettenhofer (1668–1741), had come close to this pier-section in remodelling the fifteenth-century hall-church of the Augustinians at Ebersberg east of Munich in 1733–4, and there the link with the *Sondergotik* is very obvious. This church Dominikus may have known. In contrast to the plain bases and shafts of the Steinhausen piers, moreover, stucco figures of the Latin Fathers of the Church by Anton Sturm are set before each of the coupled piers that flank the side bays, with big flower-filled urns in the same positions at the west end, and supports, so elaborate as hardly to be described as brackets, below the pulpit and the abbot's loge on either side of the choir-arch [Plates 42 and 43].

At first sight the closest similarity to Steinhausen seems to be in the handling of the zone of 'constructed decoration' between the tops of the still rigid double entablature blocks and the ceiling fresco [Plates 19 and 58]. But there are notable differences here also, differences that make Die Wies more thoroughly Rococo in spirit than Steinhausen, if not necessarily more effective visually. Except at the ends, where the frescoed Throne of Judgement and Gate of Eternity, so surprisingly simple and solid in their illusionism, rise immediately over the east and west arches, there are two zones over the arcade: one, that of the pendentives (or spandrels) immediately above the arches, is carried all around the interior; the higher is a much looser sort of frame that in fact vignettes the fresco only on the north and south sides. At the base of the lower zone the plain and still quite tectonic archivolts of the arches at Steinhausen were replaced at Die Wies by freely curved, roughly elliptical shapes broken by scrolled bosses. These are quite as devoid of structural feeling as those in Cuvilliés's Grüne Galerie of 1733 in the Munich Residenz, which may well have been their model. The actual pendentives are masqued by frescoes in *grisaille* against gold grounds set in cartouches whose shell-like edging, of the sort of advanced Rococo called *rocaille*, incorporates the boldly asymmetric flourishes common in that mode. Yet this lower zone of constructed decoration is crowned with a scallopped cornice that is relatively, as well as absolutely, heavier even than the analogous member in the Spiegelsaal of the Amalienburg [Plate 25] of some ten years earlier.

Above the coupled piers flanking the cross-axial bays the cornice carries short free-standing balustrades bowing out in front of tiny *rocaille*-framed loges that are sunk into the vignette zone [Plate 48]. In that zone, as around the cartouches below, there is not only much greater use of specifically Rococo elements, including *rocaille* detail disposed asymmetrically, but a general effect of weightlessness well beyond that of the stucco-work in the Annakapelle of 1738–40 [Plate 36] despite the actually much greater size and higher relief of the elements involved.

One must assume either that Johann Baptist collaborated on the stucco decoration here, for which as at Steinhausen there is no surviving evidence, or that Dominikus in the forties had been participating more actively in the later development of Rococo ornament in south Germany, after absorbing various new ideas from the design books of Meissonier, Cuvilliés, and others, than can be documented from his extant work. Except for his project of 1741 for the Johanniskirche in Landsberg, which we know only in the form in which the church was executed a decade later, and those for the Schongau nave and the Schussenried monastery, carried out by others after Die Wies was nearly complete, it has already been noted that there are no other recorded commissions dating from the years between the completion of Günzburg at the beginning of the decade and the consecration of the choir at Die Wies in 1749. Whatever the exact date may be of the design of the stucco-work in the nave of Die Wies, where Sturm's statues of the Latin Fathers were not installed until just before the consecration of 1754, the most extreme example of Dominikus's constructed decoration is not in the nave but over the side galleries in the choir. For this an undated and unsigned drawing [Plate 46] – presumably of *c*. 1746–8 – which Lamb attributes to Johann Baptist survives in the Städtisches Museum at Weilheim. If this attribution could be accepted it would provide strong evidence for Johann Baptist's collaboration on the stucco-work here. Although this is not at all probably by Dominikus himself, yet it seems more likely to have been drafted by one of his assistants rather than by his brother's hand – if we may judge the character of that hand from the Andechs drawing of three or four years later [Plate 49].

In front of the choir galleries mottled blue-grey scagliola columns carry tiny plain architrave blocks; but above these all sense of conventional arcuated structure is lost in the zone at the base of the barrel ceiling [Plates 45 and 57]. Dominikus's curious window-shapes, usually cut into flat wall surfaces, become here recurrent voids in relief compositions wholly made up of *rocaille* and other Rococo elements of which the primary function seems to be the vignetting of the fresco on the choir ceiling, but which also serve as screens to mask the light sources in the outer walls. The extraordinary character of this zone, tracery-like in conception, provides the climactic example of Dominikus's special achievement as a Rococo architect-decorator. It can be paralleled even in his own work only in the high altar of the Landsberg Johanniskirche [Plate 38]. This presumably dates from the time of execution of the church in the years following the completion of the choir at Die Wies, though it may just possibly have been designed as early as 1741–2.

The double altar at Die Wies, with flanking stucco figures that were installed in 1749, is rather more architecturally composed than the one at Günzburg [Plates 31 and 45]. The scagliola columns of mottled pink and white at either side are of the same order as those of the side galleries and stand on mottled blue-grey podia at the same high level. The 'arch' that joins them, although more solidly made up of bold C-scrolls than those of the side galleries, also dips in the centre as if forced down by the circular opening, invisibly lighted from behind, in which the Agnus Dei is sharply silhouetted, somewhat like the Infant Christ over the altar in the Buxheim Annakapelle [Plate 35]. Flying angels pull back to either side a gold-brocaded and fringed curtain of reddish stucco lined with blue; while overhead a scallopped and gold-pelmetted canopy of the same blue completes at this end the varied framing – elsewhere of white and gold like the stucco-work in the nave – that vignettes Johann Baptist's fresco overhead.

At the lower level of the altar, immediately behind the mensa, the miraculous Christ at the Column which brought pilgrims to Die Wies is preserved in a glazed niche framed with gilded *rocaille* ornament. This is set into a rather massive Rococo edicule of mottled grey-blue and mottled pink scagliola that is crowned by a gilded Pelican, symbolic of Christ's Sacrifice, and flanked by white stucco putti. Well above this a large oil painting of the Holy Kin by B. A. Albrecht is placed farther to the rear against the outer wall of the gallery. The keyhole shape of its frame closely resembles that of the characteristic windows Dominikus used here in the outer walls of the side galleries. Probably carved by Sturm, the gilded *rocaille* ornament of this prominent feature – more focal visually from the nave than the small figure of Christ on the altar below – echoes the generous scale of the constructed decoration in stucco over the side arches.

The Steinhausen pilgrimage was an old devotion going back even further than the fifteenth century date of the miracle-working Pietà that was set on the high altar in the new church. The Wies pilgrimage, on the other hand, was quite a new development. The cult figure is a very crude object of carved wood and cloth which was made in 1730 at the command of Abbot Gassner of Steingaden for use in the monastery's Good Friday processions. After three years it was discarded and, in 1735, given to J. M. Lori, the *Tafenwirt* (steward) of the abbey, a lay employee; he in turn gave it to his wife Maria who had a farm where is now Die Wies. On 4 May 1738 Maria Lori observed tears in the eyes of the Christ, by that time enshrined in her own room. She then had built a small stone chapel, which still stands near her house, to shelter the miraculous statue and make it accessible to others. Within four years no less than 798 votive tablets had been placed on the walls of the chapel testifying to favours granted pilgrims. On 17 March 1744, shortly after Abbot Gassner had first approached Zimmermann about building a church to accommodate the growing throngs of pilgrims, the little chapel was consecrated by permission of the Bishop of Augsburg so that mass might be said there.

At Steinhausen the fifteenth-century Pietà had suggested the particular subjects for the painted altarpiece, the fresco on the choir ceiling vault and, less directly, the Marian iconography of the painted and sculptural decoration of the nave. At Die Wies it is hard to grasp the connection between the cult figure of Christ at the Column and the painted altarpiece of the Holy Kin above it. However, on the golden books held by the outer pair of white stucco statues of the Evangelists by Egÿd I Verhelst on either side of the upper altarpiece, texts concerning the Flagellation of Christ are inscribed; while an additional inner pair of white statues of appropriate Prophets, Isaiah (equipped with a relevant text) and Malachi, call attention to the painting of the Holy Kin. Overhead, Johann Baptist's choir fresco broadens the initial theme with a representation of a cluster of flying angels carrying the Symbols of the Passion and surrounding a cloud-enthroned God the Father. Just below, the Sacrifice of Christ is again recalled by the Apocalyptic Lamb, as already by the Pelican over the lower altar.

At Steinhausen the themes represented in the nave in statuary, altar paintings and frescoes are almost entirely related to the Virgin – even such a locally significant episode as the Vision of the Premonstratensian St Hermann Joseph. Seven scenes from the Life of the Virgin are frescoed on the aisle vaults, while paintings of the Institution of the Rosary and the Death of St Joseph occupy the side altars. Her Glorification as Queen of Heaven finally dominates the whole interior as the central subject of the main ceiling fresco. Above all, however, one must be impressed by the subtlety of the visual sequence of increasing immateriality in the architecture and its decoration from the ground level, with its sturdy plain piers, to the airy fresco overhead, a sequence that is parallel, and symbolically related, to the specific iconography of the various figural paintings and sculptures.

There is a somewhat similar sequence at Die Wies. The coupled column-piers may be less bluntly material than the square ones at Steinhausen; yet the figures of the four Church Fathers are appropriately closer to the worshippers at their base than are the Apostles on top of the pillars at Steinhausen since they represent strong, once-earthly supports for the symbolic edifice of the Church. But the flower-filled urns with pairs of floating putti carrying garlands, so like those overhead in the Buxheim Annakapelle, seem wholly decorative, without particular iconographic significance.

The entablature blocks are plain and still boldly tectonic, plainer indeed than at Steinhausen though the capitals below are somewhat freer and richer [Plates 20, 42 and 43]. This makes the transition the more sudden to the constructed decoration of the pendentive zone above in which even the arches have lost their structural sense and many of the ornamental elements are of the most advanced *rocaille* character. Surprising, therefore, is the relative firmness of the scallopped cornice crowning this zone, not to speak of the literal reality of the unreachable loges with their little balconettes that open above it.

Next comes a still more startling inversion of representational expression: the vignetting frame at the sides of the fresco, which is of almost immaterial stucco-work though in three-dimensional relief, is sharply contrasted in scale and character with the rather simple and realistically conceived edicules of the Throne of

Judgement and the Gate of Eternity which are merely painted at the ends of the fresco on the cove of the ceiling [Plate 58]. In the rest of the fresco all is sky, with no reference to the earth, as in the groups of the Four Quarters of the Globe and the two Gardens at the base of the Steinhausen fresco [Plate 19]. Here banks of cloud, carrying the hierarchical hosts of Heaven, build up dome-like in aerial perspective on the flat central surface of the ceiling to the brilliant rainbow on which the Christ of the Second Coming is poised preparatory to taking His place on the Judgement Seat.

In this broader interior, with its wide central openings to left and right in the nave arcade, one is much more aware than at Steinhausen of the external walls of the nave. The big side windows with their intricate shapes and triple groupings are quite conspicuous in the smooth white walls and the crowning oculi in the diagonal bays are framed with elaborate *rocaille* stucco-work [Plate 44]. The two side altars, moreover, are as rich and strong visually as the high altar, thanks to their shining scagliola polychromy in blue-grey and pink, and nearly as tall. Thus they introduce conflicting transeptal foci outside the near-oval cylinder of coupled piers that leads up to the illusionistic vision of the open heavens overhead.

The subjects of the side altar paintings and sculptured figures have little or nothing to do with the main iconographic theme or themes. On the left the altarpiece – Christ and the Magdalen by J. G. Bergmüller (1688–1762) (head of the Augsburg Akademie) – is flanked by white-painted wooden figures of the Magdalen and St Margaret of Cortona, with Abraham above, by Sturm. On the right, the Repentance of Peter, painted by the Tyrolean-born Joseph Magges (1728–69), is flanked by Sturm's figures of Sts Norbert and Bernard of Clairvaux, with Divine Wisdom above. Though not entirely completed until 1759, five years after the consecration of the church, these side altars must have been an integral part of Zimmermann's final plans, and Bergmüller, in executing them, will have followed Dominikus Zimmermann's designs as closely as did Dominikus's old associate Pontian Steinhauser and his sons in executing the pulpit and the abbot's loge, both notable masterpieces of German Rococo church-furniture.

This very brief account of Die Wies, concerning which more has probably been written than about any other single Rococo church, may well end on a more personal note. In 1750 one of Dominikus's four sons, Franz Dominikus, who was supervising the construction of the church, married the widowed Maria Lori and together they thenceforth ran an inn at Die Wies to house pilgrims. In March 1754 Dominikus (whose wife had died two years earlier) began to sell his property in Landsberg. In 1757, after selling more Landsberg property, he dedicated a votive painting at Die Wies, executed in oil with pathetic incompetence by himself, in gratitude for the successful completion of the church. It is said that Dominikus wished to settle at Steinhausen when he retired but was discouraged from doing so by the Schussenried monks who controlled the Steinhausen church. In 1748 he had been commissioned to plan a new church and monastery for Schussenried, as has been noted earlier, and of this a model was made the next year [Plate 49]. But after the death of Father Thaddäus (Dominikus's son Georg's name in religion) the other monks decided, presumably for economy's sake, to entrust the reconstruction of their monastery to the local architect, Jakob Emele, who had long before been one of Zimmermann's assistants at Steinhausen. The then abbot, Siard Frick, was only too well aware how high the cost could be of employing Dominikus since he had been responsible, after Abbot Ströbele's demission in 1733, for completing the furnishing of Steinhausen; indeed, the high altar was only just being installed there in 1750, the year of Frick's death. So Dominikus, instead of retiring to Steinhausen, built a small house that still stands close to the front of the church at Die Wies [Plate 41] and there he was living at the time of his death in 1766.

Die Wies was Dominikus's last major work though he lived for a decade after its completion. Something, however, has already been said of Eresing (1755–7) and of Gutenzell (1755–62), where his daughter became abbess in 1759 (pp. 35–6). What still deserves mention is his Johanniskirche in Landsberg, designed in 1741, halted in 1742 by the War of the Austrian Succession, and later carried to completion contemporaneously with Die Wies in 1750–52. A fairly small oval in plan with a circular choir, it has three features that should be specifically noted: the façade, the high altar, and the oval oculus above the choir arch which links the dome of the nave with that of the choir, a device premonitory of the holes above the choir arcades at Die Wies – if it was, in fact, already proposed in the project of 1741.

The façade is modest in height and, for all its horizontal entablature, takes its place comfortably among the plain gabled houses along the street [Plate 37]. The canted pilasters and flanking concavities on either side of the entrance recall the transeptal treatment inside the Günzburg church and, ultimately, Borromini's side façade of the Propaganda Fide in Rome. Because of that strong Roman echo, it can hardly be considered Rococo rather than Baroque; but it is certainly as different from the plastic convexity of the façade of Die Wies, with its giant columns and its curving crown, as from the flat walls, relieved by very slight curves in plan, the thin pilasters, and the painted band-work of Steinhausen, Günzburg, and the flanks of Die Wies.

The scagliola high altar is very remarkable, even though the figural group of the Baptism of Christ by Johann Luidl and the landscape fresco behind by the local painter K. J. Thalheimer (1712–99) are both of rather low quality [Plate 38]. Zimmermann designed it entirely without conventional architectural elements and very much in the spirit of the constructed decoration over the sides of the choir at Die Wies. But here the smooth scagliola surfaces and the very pale colouring suggest that Dominikus may have been consciously imitating porcelain, as Johann Baptist perhaps set out to do in his side altars of 1748 in the chapel of the Munich Residenz, to judge at least from their present heavily restored condition. Imitation of porcelain, it will be noted, comes late (if at all) in the story of German Rococo architecture, not early as has sometimes been supposed. Generally, German porcelain imitated architecture, or at least published designs such as Meissonier's and Cuvilliés's, not the other way round, and continued to do so well after the Rococo had been superseded in architectural design and decoration.

But Dominikus must also have been seeking here to rival the Berninian altarpieces of the Asams, as he had done in a modest way with the Infant Christ above the corona in the Annakapelle at Buxheim in the late 1730s and with the Agnus Dei over the upper altar at Die Wies in the late forties. The crudity of the execution of the fresco, with its implausible clouds carried up over the entablature of the choir behind a Dove suspended in a three-dimensional glory, sadly diminishes the effectiveness of the intended illusion and contrasts unhappily with the virtuoso handling of the *rocaille* elements of the scagliola frame. Yet this altar is one of the few instances where decorative work for which Dominikus was alone responsible almost rivals the more elegant and sophisticated productions of his brother. But Dominikus had, of course, begun his artistic career as a designer of scagliola altars [Plate 2].

Although Johann Baptist died in 1758, eight years before Dominikus, he was very busy indeed in the last decade of his life. As has been noted, his redecoration with stucco-work and frescoes of St-Blasius in Landshut, which he undertook in the late 1740s, is not very successful. Concerning his work at Andechs of 1751–5 enough has been said already (pp. 33–5), as also perhaps about the Nymphenburg Great Hall of 1756–7 (p. 33). Johann Baptist's work in St-Peter in Munich of 1753–6 was very largely destroyed in the war as was his stuccoed ceiling in Cuvilliés's

Residenz Theater of 1752–5. But he also worked in the 1750s at three large churches: Maria Brunnlein outside Wemding in 1752–4, a belated wall-pillar church built over the years 1748–52 by F. J. Roth; Schäftlarn; and the Neustift at Freising, remodelled after a fire by J. M. Fischer in the mid-fifties. Of these it may be sufficient to describe in conclusion the finest, Schäftlarn, since the other two remain essentially Baroque despite the profusion of their Rococo decoration in fresco and stucco.

Johann Baptist, in the early part of his career, had served chiefly the Benedictines, and in the 1750s at Andechs a Benedictine monastery was again his employer. But from Steinhausen on his most important clients, other than the Munich court, had been the Premonstratensians. At Schäftlarn, as at Freising Neustift, where he was active in 1754–6, just before his late work at Freising and at Nymphenburg, the life of the twelfth-century founder of the Premonstratensian Order, St Norbert, and the history of the monastery itself provided the subjects for the ceiling frescoes.

As in other late commissions – he was seventy-four when he undertook the decoration of Schäftlarn – he had the assistance of his son Franz Michael. The frescoes are especially large in the middle bay of the nave and in the choir. Moreover, their rather plain and solid frames fit down so firmly over the arches below the handkerchief vaults that they constrict the big cartouches in the pendentives with their modest *grisaille* paintings [Plate 51]. In alternation with the large frescoes, those in the first and third bays of the nave and in the apse are loosely vignetted by stucco borders of *rocaille* ornament. All the frescoes are exceptionally light and bright in tone as well as notably open and aerial; this is especially evident as one looks from east to west. In the other direction the solid ground and the architectural setting of the fresco of the Founding of the Abbey in the middle nave bay, with the feathery landscape on the right recalling the location of the church in the Isar valley, is echoed in the symmetrical *quadratura* edifice, open and tree-flanked though it is, from within which, as just after this in the choir of Freising Neustift, the Virgin presents a scapulary to St Norbert.

But if the frescoes of Schäftlarn, even more than those of the Nymphenburg Festsaal [Plate 53], bring the career of J. B. Zimmermann as a painter to a brilliant conclusion, the delicate stucco decoration, so unusually restrained in quantity and formal in its distribution, suggests a close collaboration with the architect such as seems for some reason to have been lacking at Maria Brunnlein, and which was impossible in Viscardi's vigorously Baroque interior of the Neustift even when Fischer was restoring it. The question is: who was the architect with whom Zimmermann collaborated here? For the building history of Schaftlarn is a complicated one.

Begun in 1733 by Cuvilliés the construction, which was supervised by Franz Ronninger, first dragged and then came to a stop after 1740 with the outbreak of the War of the Austrian Succession. When activity was renewed in 1751 not Cuvilliés but Gunetzrhainer, his superior as *Oberhofbaumeister* in Munich as Effner had been earlier, was in charge, but he was assisted by a 'Herr Fischer'. Presumably this was J. M. Fischer, who had married Gunetzrhainer's step-sister in 1725, and with whom Zimmermann had already worked at Ingolstadt and at Berg-am-Laim in the 1730s and 40s. Melchior Streicher (†1772), who had been assisting Fischer on the Anastasiakapelle at Benedikt-beuern, supervised. Considering the happy results of Zimmer-mann's collaboration in secular work with Cuvilliés, beginning a quarter century before this and lately renewed in the Residenz (now Cuvilliés) Theater, the results here might suggest – were it not contradicted by the documents – that Zimmermann worked with him at Schäftlarn. The former's much earlier association with Gunetzrhainer at Seligenthal had certainly produced no such harmoniously ordered interior.

The Ingolstadt church which Zimmermann frescoed for Fischer in 1740 is destroyed; but photographs indicate some points of similarity with Schäftlarn in the great size of the nave fresco and the way its heavily reeded and garlanded frame fits down over the pendentives, not to speak of the general restraint of the stucco-work, whether or not this was executed by Zim-mermann. At Berg-am-Laim, however, where the decorations were only completed by Zimmermann a good ten years after the original project was prepared in 1735, there is a certain amount of discord between the distinctly Baroque character of most of the architectural elements – engaged columns, tall regularly shaped clerestory windows, and tectonically framed niches – and the *rocaille* detail of the stucco-work. The stucco-work almost seems here an afterthought not foreseen by the architect as in several of Fischer's other major churches. The personal taste of the church's patron, Clemens August, elector of Cologne, may be the explana-tion at Berg-am-Laim, or the fact that it was partly built not by Fischer but by P. J. Köglsperger (b. 1707), who modified Fischer's design for the façade.

It is not clear – was perhaps not yet even decided by Fischer and his clients – who was expected to execute the stucco ornament indicated on the clerestory and vaults in a sectional drawing of Ottobeuren, thought to be of *c.* 1748, which is preserved in the monastery's archive. That drawing, however, provides rather stronger evidence than Ingolstadt for presuming it was with

Fischer that Zimmermann collaborated at Schäftlarn. In it one finds the same consistent use of broad plain areas of wall and vault outlined by rather thin lines of Rococo detailing. Instead of free and bold swatches of *rocaille* – present in varying degree of profusion in Zimmermann's slightly earlier work at Wemding and just after this in the Neustift and at Nymphenburg – in the drawing and at Schäftlarn straight mouldings frame the various surfaces, while the richer ornament is largely confined, as in the Early Rococo of Pierre Lepautre, to the ends and middles of panels [Plates 51 and 52]. The effect is not yet dry, as it would be ten years later in Fischer's Altomünster and at Gutenzell [Plate 55]. On the other hand, there is no smothering of the architectural forms with an excess of decoration as at Fischer's Diessen in the late thirties and, *a fortiori*, at Ottobeuren as executed, where J. M. Feuchtmayr's campaign of decoration began in 1756 just as Zimmermann's at Schäftlarn was ending.

This sort of relatively late Rococo decoration suits especially well the generous coved chamfers, so characteristic of Fischer, which are used at Schäftlarn at both ends of the nave, in the shallow transeptal projections, and at smaller scale round the windows [Plate 52]. The resultant emphasis on continuity of surface, which is sustained by the flatness of the broad ribs between the bays, makes up for the relatively tectonic – and hence un-Rococo – treatment of the wall-pillars. But the projection of the entablatures of the wall-pillars is much reduced, nor do these continue across the side walls where the big round windows open. The pilasters, moreover, are so shallow in relief that they barely break the wall-surfaces, unlike the fluted pilasters at Ingolstadt or the engaged columns that Fischer used so conspicuously at Zwiefalten. Such are employed here only at the sides of the altars that J. B. Straub (1704–84) carried out over the years 1756–64 after Zimmermann's work was completed. The result is an interior surprisingly unitary in spirit, successfully rivalling the more theatrical effects and the complex architectural and decorative symbolism of Dominikus Zimmermann's Steinhausen and Die Wies to which Johann Baptist had also made such especially important contributions.

But even in Germany the end of the Rococo was not far off now: in 1756 the highly critical *Essai* of the French Abbé Laugier was translated into German and Neo-Classicism was on the way. Even so, fine Rococo interiors continued to be produced for a decade and more by younger men than the Zimmermanns.

Bibliographical Note

The amount of writing in German on German Baroque and Rococo architecture over the last eighty years since Cornelius Gurlitt's *Barock und Rokoko Architektur* appeared in Berlin in 1889, covering the subject seriously for the first time, has been voluminous, but material in English is scarce. The following list is intended to include all the English titles specifically concerned with the subject, but for German titles it is much more selective. Monographs on individual buildings are entered only in the Notes to the illustrations (pp. 85–94) and monographic literature on the Zimmermann's contemporaries is not included at all. Various good books exist, of course, on the Germans, J. B. Neumann, J. M. Fischer, the brothers Asam, and Dominikus's reputed followers, the Dossenbergers, among many others less relevant here. There are also reliable books on the Austrians, J. B. Fischer von Erlach and Johann Lukas von Hildebrandt. Moreover, the useful post-war editions of Dehio's *Handbücher der deutschen Kunstdenkmäler*, occasionally referred to in the Notes to the illustrations, as revised by E. Gall and the volumes of *Reclams Kunstführer* for south-eastern Germany deserve mention here.

ITEMS IN ENGLISH

ON DOMINIKUS ZIMMERMANN:

Standish D. Lawder, *The Structure of the Inner Lining in the Churches of Dominikus Zimmermann*, Yale University Master's Thesis, 1962 (unpublished).

S. Lane Faison, 'Dominikus Zimmermann', *Magazine of Art*, XLV, 1952, pp. 269 ff.

GENERAL WORKS:

Sacheverell Sitwell, *German Baroque Art*, (London, 1927).

W. H. Bruford, *Germany in the Eighteenth Century*, (Cambridge, 1935).

Fiske Kimball, *The Creation of the Rococo*, (Philadelphia: Philadelphia Museum of Art, 1943; London: Oldbourne, 1964; French ed., Paris, 1949).

T. H. B. Burrough, *South German Baroque*, (London: Tiranti, 1956).

Nicolas Powell, *From Baroque to Rococo*, (London: Faber & Faber, 1959).

John Bourke, *Baroque Churches of Central Europe*, 2nd ed., (London: Faber & Faber, 1962).

Eberhard Hempel, *Baroque Art and Architecture in Central Europe*, (Harmondsworth: Penguin, 1965).

H.-R. Hitchcock, *Rococo Architecture Studies*, (London: Phaidon Press, 1968).

ITEMS IN GERMAN

ON THE ZIMMERMANNS:

T. Muchall-Viebrook, *Dominikus Zimmermann*, (Leipzig, 1912).

N. Worobiow, *Die Fensterformen Dominikus Zimmermanns*, Munich University Doctoral Dissertation, 1934.

J. B. Schmid, 'Johann Baptist Zimmermann, Maler und kurfürstlichbayerischer Hofstuccateur', *Altbayerische Monatschrift*, 1900, Heft 1–5.

E. Günther, *Die Brüder Zimmermann*, (Königsberg, 1944).

C. Thon, *J. B. Zimmermann*, Mainz University Doctoral Dissertation, (? *c.* 1965).

GENERAL WORKS:

M. Hauttmann, *Geschichte der kirchlichen Baukunst in Bayern, Schwaben und Franken*, 1550–1780, (Munich-Berlin-Leipzig, 1921).

A. Feulner, *Bayerisches Rokoko*, (Munich, 1923).

H. M. Schnell, *Der Baierische Barock*, (Munich, 1942).

N. Lieb, *Barockkirchen zwischen Donau und Alpen*, (Munich, 1958).

H. W. Hegemann, *Deutsches Rokoko*, (Königstein-im-Taunus, 1958).

G. Barthel, *Barockkirchen in Altbayern und Schwaben*, (Munich-Berlin, n.d.).

B. Rupprecht, *Die bayerische Rokoko-Kirche*, (Kallmünz, 1959).

J. Le Brun and P. Sufermeister, *Barocke Welt*, (Berne and Stuttgart, 1966).

Plates

1   Edelstetten, Frauenstift Church, 1709–10, interior to east.
     [*Hermann Hessler*]

2　Buxheim, Carthusian Church, 1711–13, interior to east. [*Cramers Kunstanstalt*]

3   Buxheim, Carthusian Church, 1711–13, choir vault. [*Dr Fritz Arens*]

5   Mödingen, Dominican Nunnery Church, 1716–18, interior to west.
[*Hermann Hessler*]

7   Landsberg-am-Lech, Rathaus, 1720.

8   Schleissheim, Great Hall, 1723–4. [*Helga Schmidt-Glassner*]

9   Schleissheim, Kammerkapelle, 1724–5, ceiling. [*Helga Schmidt-Glassner*]

11   Buxheim, Parish Church, [?]1726–7. [*Dr Fritz Arens*]

12   Buxheim, Parish Church, [?]1726–7, interior to east.
[Dr Fritz Arens]

13   First project for Pilgrimage Church, Steinhausen, 1727, plan.
      [*Foto Hütter*]

14   Steinhausen, Pilgrimage Church, 1728–33, transverse section.
      [from *Kunstdenkmäler von Württemberg*, 1943]

15   Steinhausen, Pilgrimage Church, 1728–33, plan.
      [from Carl Lamb, *Die Wies*, Berlin, 1937]

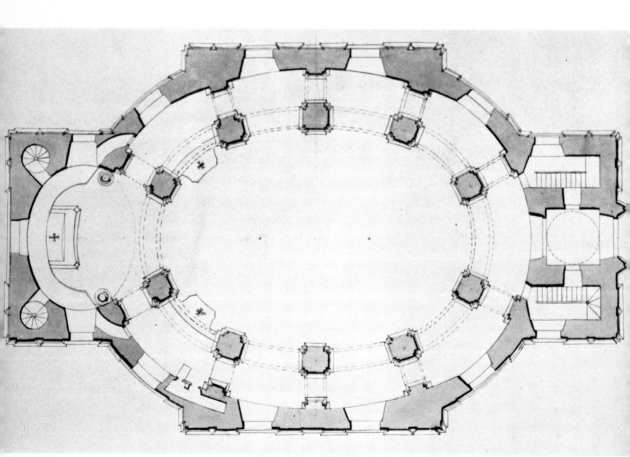

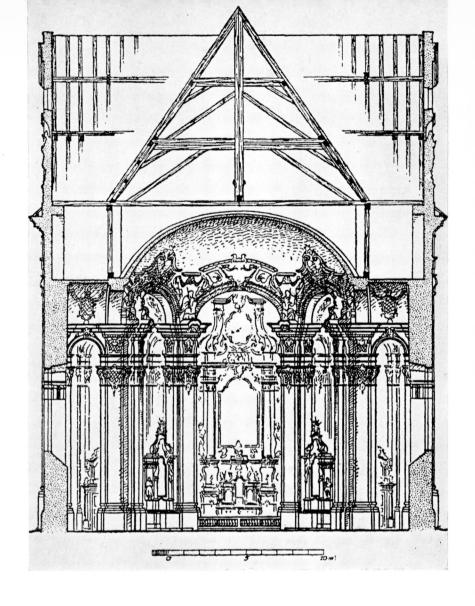

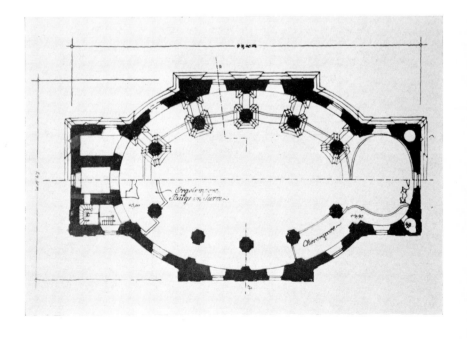

16   Steinhausen, Pilgrimage Church, 1728–33. [*Lala Aufsberg*]

17   Steinhausen, Pilgrimage Church, 1728–33, interior to east.
   [*Hirmer Foto-Archiv*]

18 Steinhausen, Pilgrimage Church, 1728–33, interior to west.
   [*A. Mauthe*]

19 Steinhausen, Pilgrimage Church, 1728–33, looking upward.
   [*Hirmer Foto-Archiv*]

20 Steinhausen, Pilgrimage Church, 1728–33, pilaster capitals.
   [*Georg Dangel*]

21 Weyarn, Augustinian Abbey Church, 1729, to east. [*Dr Johannes Steiner*]

22 Munich, Residenz, Schatzkammer, 1731–3. [*Staatliche Schlösser, Gärten und Seen*]

23 Benediktbeuern, Benedictine Abbey,
Neuer Festsaal, 1731–2. [*Dr Johannes Steiner*]

24 Project for Ottobeuren Abbey Church, 1732, plan.
[from Lieb, *Barockkirchen*, Munich, 1958]

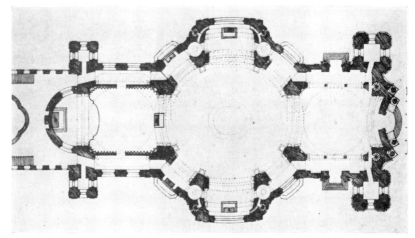

27   Prien, Parish Church, 1735–8, interior to east. [*Lala Aufsberg*]

28   Prien, Parish Church, 1735–8, interior to west. [*Lala Aufsberg*]

29   Günzburg, Parish Church, 1736–41, plan.
   [from Carl Lamb, *Die Wies*, Berlin, 1937]

30   Günzburg, Parish Church, 1736–41, exterior.
   [*Deutscher Kunstverlag*]

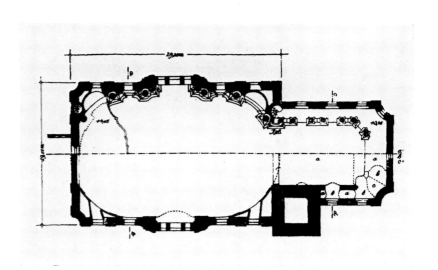

31 Günzburg, Parish Church, 1736–41, interior to east.
[*Dr Johannes Steiner*]

32 Günzburg, Parish Church, 1736–41, interior to west.
[*Dr Johannes Steiner*]

33   Günzburg, Parish Church, 1736–41, transverse section of choir.
[from Carl Lamb, *Die Wies*, Berlin, 1937]

34   Günzburg, Parish Church, 1736–41, choir. [*Dr Johannes Steiner*]

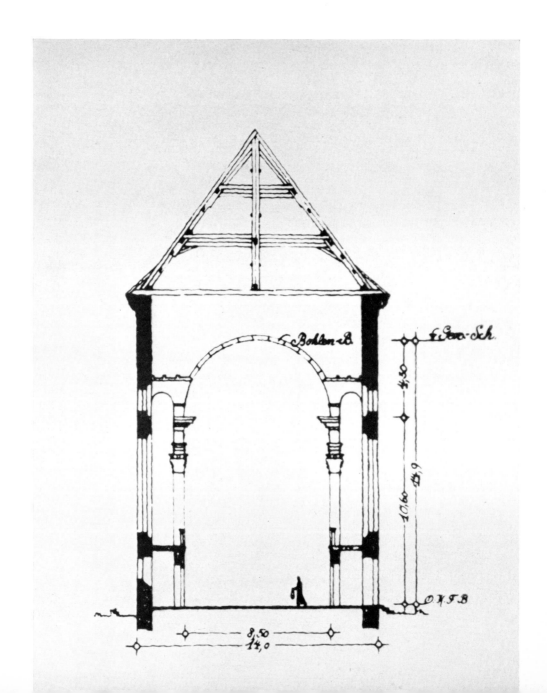

35   Buxheim, Carthusian Monastery, Annakapelle, 1738–40, altar.
[*Lala Aufsberg*]

36 Buxheim, Carthusian Monastery, Annakapelle, 1738–40, vault.
[*Lala Aufsberg*]

37   Landsberg-am-Lech, Johanniskirche, 1750–52, exterior.
     [*Bildarchiv Foto Marburg*]

38   Landsberg-am-Lech, Johanniskirche, high altar, *c*.1741 or *c*.1751.
     [*Dr Johannes Steiner*]

39   First project for Die Wies, Pilgrimage Church, *c.*1744–5, plan.
     [from Carl Lamb, *Die Wies*, Berlin, 1937]

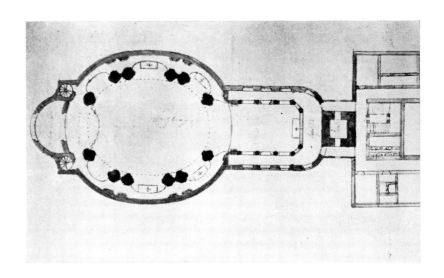

40   Die Wies, Pilgrimage Church, 1746–54, plan.
     [from Carl Lamb, *Die Wies*, Berlin, 1937]

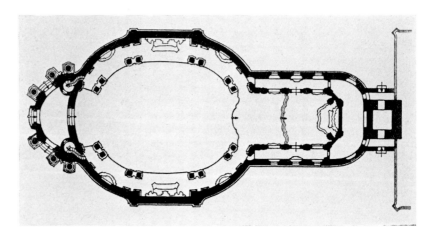

41   Die Wies, Pilgrimage Church, 1746–54. [*Peter Keetman*]

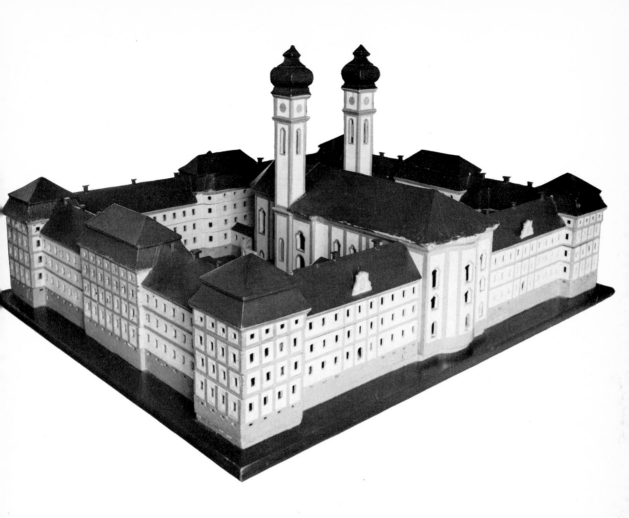

46   Project for Premonstratensian Abbey, Schussenried, 1748–9, model.
[*Foto Hütter*]

47   Andechs, Benedictine Abbey, Church, 1751–5, plan.
     [*Verlag Schnell und Steiner*]

48   Andechs, Benedictine Abbey, Church, 1751–5, interior to east.
     [*Dr Johannes Steiner*]

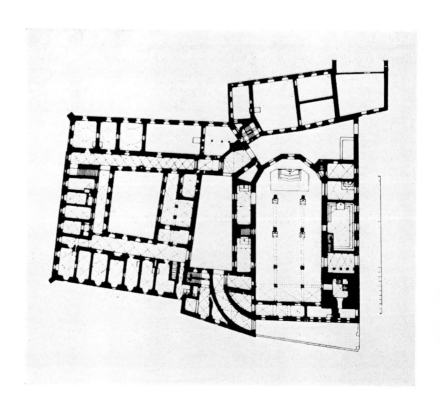

49   Project for east end, Andechs, 1751
     [from Bauerreis and Schnell, *Der Heilige Berg Andechs*, Munich, 1955]

50   Andechs, Benedictine Monastery, Church, 1751–5, west end.
[*Dr Johannes Steiner*]

51   Schäftlarn, Premonstratensian Abbey, Church, 1754–6, interior to east.
[*Hirmer Foto-Archiv*]

52   Schäftlarn, Premonstratensian Abbey, Church, 1754–6, interior to north.
[*Hirmer Foto-Archiv*]

53 Nymphenburg, Schloss, Great Hall, 1755–7.
[*Hirmer Foto-Archiv*]

54 Nymphenburg, Schloss, Music Gallery, 1755–7.
[*Hirmer Foto-Archiv*]

55   Gutenzell, Cistercian Nunnery, Church, 1755–63, interior to east. [*Georg Dangel*]

56   Project for 'constructed decoration' in choir, Die Wies, *c.* 1746–8.
      [*Haus Pfaffenwinkel, Weilheim*]

57   Die Wies, Pilgrimage Church, choir, 1746–9, gallery. [*Hirmer Foto-Archiv*]

Notes on the Plates

1. EDELSTETTEN (nr Krumbach), Frauenstift Church. Designed, 1709, by Father Christoph Vogt (1648–1725), and built, 1710, by Simpert Krämer (1679–1753).

Interior, with stucco decoration in white and frescoes, 1710, by J. B. Z.; altars of *c.* 1710, the high altar incorporating an Assumption of the Virgin, dated 1660 but unsigned; and pulpit dated 1728.

Ernst Gall, *Handbuch der deutschen Kunstdenkmäler. Östliches Schwaben*, (Munich, 1954), p. 138.

2–3. BUXHEIM (nr Memmingen), Carthusian Monastery Church. Choir of *c.* 1300; nave after 1402; screen of 1512; the whole remodelled 1690.

Interior, as renewed for Prior Petrus Leikard, 1711–13, with white stucco decoration on pale blue and yellow grounds by D. Z. surrounding frescoes – (from E to W) the Glorification of the Sacred Heart, the Pentecost, St John Baptist Preaching, St Bruno called to Rome, and other Carthusian episodes – by J. B. Z., one of which is signed and dated 1711; mottled grey scagliola altars by D. Z. incorporating paintings by unknown artists of (N) the Mass of St Bruno and (S) the Mystic Marriage of St Catherine, flanked by figures of Sts Hugh of Grenoble and Hugh of Lincoln and Sts Barbara and Ursula, respectively, by (?) J. G. Reusch; and high altar by Sigmund Schalk, 1631, with painting of the Assumption of the Virgin by J. G. Bergmüller (1688–1762), 1718.

Fritz Arens and Friedrich Stöhlker, *Die Kartäuse Buxheim*, (Buxheim, 1962).

4. OTTOBEUREN (nr Memmingen), Benedictine Abbey.

Planned and begun, 1711, by Father Vogt and carried out by Hans II Brenner (1676–1749) to 1717 for Abbot Rupert II Ness.

Library, with pinkish scagliola columns and gilt capitals, 1715, and white stucco decoration on pale pink and green grounds, 1716–18, by J. B. Z. surrounding frescoes of the Arrival of St Benedict at Monte Cassino, etc., commissioned, 1716, from Elias Zobel and completed by Arbogast Thalheimer; statue of Athena, *c.* 1725, by (?) Anton Sturm (1690–1757).

Hugo Schnell, *Ottobeuren, Kirche, Kloster, Museum*, 4th ed., (Munich, 1962).

Norbert Lieb, 'Die barocke Architektur und Bildwelt des Stifts Ottobeuren', in *Ottobeuren, Festschrift zur 1200–Jahrefeier der Abtei*, (Augsburg, 1964), pp. 334–6.

5. MÖDINGEN (nr Dillingen), Dominican Nunnery Church. Built 1716–18 (consecrated 25 August 1721) by D. Z. for Prioress Magdalena von Stein zu Rechtenstein, with stucco-work by D. Z., dated MDCCXIIX (1718) over the choir arch, and frescoes by J. B. Z., one of which is signed and dated 1719 and another 1722. Nave 20·85 × 13·30 m, choir 14·10 × 8·50 m. Cost 37,358 gulden.

Interior to west, with white stucco decoration on pale yellow, green, and pink fields and natural-coloured garlands; frescoes of St Thomas Aquinas, the Latin Fathers of the Church, and the Mystic Marriage of St Catherine by J. B. Z.; nuns' choir on balcony and organ gallery above.

6. Exterior of convent, built 1720–29 by D. Z.; cost 20,365 gulden.

Julius Schöttl, *Kloster Maria-Medingen* (Kunstführer 509) 2nd ed., (Munich, 1961). (In later Notes others of the small Kunstführer published by Schnell & Steiner are given by number and date and not by author and title.)

7. LANDSBERG-AM-LECH, Rathaus. Erected 1699–1702.

Stucco decoration, mostly in white, on façade by D. Z., 1720; ground storey and gable modified, 1863, the probable date of the present colours: deep pink below, lighter pink and green above.

Ernst Gall, *Handbuch der deutschen Kunstdenkmäler. Oberbayern*, 3rd ed., (Munich, 1960), p. 277.

8. SCHLEISSHEIM (nr Munich), Neues Schloss. Designed, 1692–3, and begun, 1701–4, by Enrico Zuccalli (*c.* 1642–1724) for Elector Max Emanuel (1679–1726); carried further, 1719–26, by Josef Effner (1687–1745) for Max Emanuel, with modifications related to a project of 1714 by Robert de Cotte (1656–1735); still further modified and completed, 1847–9, for King Ludwig I to plans by Leo von Klenze (1784–1864), made in 1819 for King Max I; damaged by bombing, 1944, and since largely restored.

Festsaal by Effner, 1723–4, with stucco decoration in white by

C. C. Dubut (1687–1742) and J. B. Z.; ceiling fresco of Aeneas and Turnus by Jacopo Amigoni (1675–1752); and large oil paintings, dated 1702–4, of Relief of Vienna and Defeat of the Turks in Hungary by F. J. Beich (1665–1748) in white and gold frames.

9. Kammerkapelle by (?) Effner, with plaster ceiling, 1724–5, in gold on white by J. B. Z. and ceiling painting, 1726, by N. G. Stuber (1688–1749), above early seventeenth-century pink and grey scagliola walls brought from the Munich Residenz and extended by J. G. Baader (b. 1692).

Luisa Hager, *Schloss Schleissheim* (Grosse Baudenkmäler Heft 94), (Berlin, 1945); idem., *Schleissheim*, (Konigstein-im-Taunus, 1964); Max Hauttmann, *Der kurbayerische Hofbaumeister Joseph Effner*, (Strasbourg, 1913), pp. 106–44.

10. BENEDIKTBEUERN (nr Bad Tölz), Benedictine Abbey. Library (now school refectory) built as separate structure in 1722–4 by Josef Hainz (?–1763), probably from designs by Michael Ötschmann (1670–1755), for Abbot Magnus Pachinger. Stucco decoration in creamy pale beige on white ground, and frescoes, badly needing cleaning, of the Benedictine Order as Supporter of Ancient Culture and Allegory of the Sciences, etc., signed and dated 1725, by J. B. Z.

Karl Mindera, *Benediktbeuern*, (Munich, 1957).

11. BUXHEIM (nr Memmingen), Parish Church. Built by D. Z. (?)1726–7. Exterior.

12. Interior to east, with white stucco decoration on pale yellow, green, and pink grounds by D. Z.; ceiling fresco in choir of Nativity, dated 1727, by F. G. Hermann (1692–1769); altars of dark brown with mottled green scagliola columns, also of 1727, by G. D. Weis, incorporating (N) a terracottta Madonna of *c.* 1420, (E) Christ and St Peter by Hermann between statues of Sts Joseph and John Baptist by Anton Sturm (1690–1757), and (S) a statue of St Barbara by Sturm.

Fritz Arens and Friedrich Stöhlker, *Die Kartäuse Buxheim*, (Buxheim, 1962).

13. STEINHAUSEN (nr Biberach), Pilgrimage and Parish Church. Commissioned, 1727, and built, 1728–33 (consecrated 5 May 1733) by D. Z., assisted by Hans Michael Köpf, Kaspar and Georg Finsterwalder, Jakob Emele (1706–80) and others, with frescoes of 1730–31 by J. B. Z., assisted by his sons Joseph (1707–43) and possibly Franz Michael (1709–84), for Abbot Didacus Ströbele of the Premonstratensian Monastery of Schussenried. Cost 48,495 gulden. Nave $25 \cdot 50 \times 14 \cdot 50$ m, with aisle $1 \cdot 80$ m wide; choir $7 \cdot 60 \times 11 \cdot 20$ m; height at crown of dome $19 \cdot 50$ m.

First project, 1727 (plan now preserved in the Bürgerbibliotek, Lucerne).

14, 15. Section and plan.

16. Exterior from south-west, with pink walls and pale green pilaster order.

17. Interior to east, with white stucco decoration including many touches of gold and pale pink and some gold *mosaïque* by D. Z., assisted by Nikolaus Schütz (†1785), Pontian Steinhauser, and others; fully polychromed figures of the Apostles over the piers by D. Z., commissioned in 1730; fresco of the Fountain of Life, 1730–31 by J. B. Z.; high altar to D. Z.'s original design, executed, 1749–50, by Joachim Früholzer in near-black scagliola with mottled columns, gilded capitals, etc., and incorporating a large oil-painted Deposition and an Ascension above by F. M. Kuen (1719–71), behind the sculptured Pietà of *c.* 1415, which is the principal object of devotion, and white-painted carved wooden figures of Sts Peter, Paul, Gabriel and Michael; side altars, 1746, by Früholzer, of similar colouring including painting of (N) the Institution of the Rosary and (S) the Death of St Joseph by Josef Esperlin (1707–75), and carved figures of (N) Sts Joachim and Anna and (S) Sts Maurice and Sebastian; and pulpit of 1732–4 by J. G. Prestel, as remodelled in 1746 by Früholzer.

18. Interior to west, with organ-gallery, and organ-case by J. G. Reusch, 1732–3.

19. Detail of nave, with fresco by J. B. Z. of the Virgin as Queen of Heaven above the Garden of Eden and two of the Four Continents; stucco figures of the Apostles by D. Z.; and pulpit by Prestel and Früholzer.

20. Pilaster capitals, of white stucco with gilded highlights and pink and green fields.

Alfons Kasper and Wolf Strache, *Steinhausen, ein Juwel unter den Dorfkirchen*, (Stuttgart, 1957); Norbert Lieb, *Barockkirchen zwischen Donau and Alpen*, 2nd ed., (Munich, 1958), pp. 111–18, 161–2, 172 (Bibl., p. 162), henceforth cited merely as Lieb, *Barockkirchen*; Wolf Strache, *Steinhausen, ein Lobgesang in Bildern*, (Stuttgart, 1958); Kunstführer 203, 2nd ed., (Munich, 1960).

21. WEYARN (on Autobahn E-11), Augustinian Abbey Church. Built 1687–93 by Lorenzo Sciascia (1643–94) for Prior Gelasius Harlass. Interior to east, with stucco decorations partly gilded, partly in delicate naturalistic colours against white, pale grey, and blue-green grounds, with some gold *mosaïque*; and frescoes on the nave ceiling of St Augustine and of the Founding of the Abbey, signed and dated 1729, by J. B. Z., undertaken in preparation for the 600th anniversary of the founding of the abbey in 1733; high altar of 1693, incorporating a painting of Christ and St Peter by J. B. Untersteiner (†1713), and a tabernacle, 1763, by Ignaz Günther (1725–75) flanked by figures

of Sts Ambrose and Augustine; at east end of nave (N) Annunciation and (S) Pietà groups by Günther, 1764; side altars of c. 1700; (S) the Shrine of St Valerius with angels by Günther, 1763; and (N) the pulpit of 1699.

Kunstführer 612, 4th ed., (Munich, 1962).

22. MUNICH, Residenz. Schatzkammer (now Porzellan-kabinett) executed, 1731–3, by François Cuvilliés (1695–1768) for Elector Carl Albrecht with gold on white ceiling decoration by J. B. Z, above *boiseries* by Joachim Dietrich (†1753).

Hans Thoma, *Residenzmuseum München*, (Munich, 1960), pp. 13–14, 23.

23. BENEDIKTBEUERN (nr Bad Tölz), Benedictine Abbey. West wing built by Hainz from designs of Ötschmann, 1728–31, for Abbot Pachinger.

Neuer Festsaal (now chapel of Salesian school), with largely monochrome stucco decoration, barely touched with gold, and frescoes of a Benedictine Robing Scene, the Elements, and the Season by J. B. Z., 1731–2, assisted by his son Joseph.

Karl Mindera, *Benediktbeuern*, (Munich, 1957), pp. 33–5.

24. PROJECT for Ottobeuren Abbey Church, 1732. (Plan preserved in Ottobeuren Klosterarchiv.)

Lieb, *Barokkirchen*, p. 158.

25. NYMPHENBURG (nr Munich), Amalienburg. Built 1734–9, by Cuvilliés for the Elector Carl Albrecht. J. B. Z. received 2,518 florins by contract for the interior stucco-work and a further 234 florins for work on the façade and the model for a garden urn.

Spiegelsaal, with stucco decoration by J. B. Z. in silvered relief on light-blue (originally milk-white) ground above *boiseries* by Dietrich.

26. Fishery group on ceiling by J. B. Z.

Luisa Hager, *Nymphenburg*, (Munich, n.d.), pp. 44–53, idem., *Nymphenburg*, (Königstein-im-Taunus, 1964), pl. 20–29.

27. PRIEN (on Chiemsee), Parish Church. Built, 1735–8, by Johann Steinpeisz.

Interior to east, with stucco decoration in grey and gold on white grounds, with much gold *mosaïque*, ceiling frescoes (in choir) of the Trinity and (in eastern corners of nave) of patron saints of the daughter-churches of Prien, 1738, by J. B. Z.; marble altar-rail and altars by Georg Dobler, 1738–40, with sculpture by P. Mödlhammer, 1742; stucco angels above high altar, small paintings and brilliant blue stucco draperies above dark scagliola side altars by J. B. Z. (The large altar paintings are of nineteenth-century date.)

28. Interior to west, with fresco of Battle of Lepanto, signed and dated 1738, by J. B. Z.; scagliola pulpit by J. B. Z., 1739;

and organ-case by Georg Anton Kidl, 1739.

Ernst Gall, *Handbuch der deutschen Kunstdenkmäler. Oberbayern*, 3rd ed., (Munich, 1960), p. 427.

29. GÜNZBURG, Parish Church. Built, 1736–41, by D. Z., assisted by Johann Michael Krepp, Pontian Steinhauser and Michael Köpf, for Town Council; restored 1902–3 and 1951–2. D. Z.'s estimate of cost 13,129 gulden. Nave 27×18·50 m and *c.* 20 m high in centre; choir 13 × 3·50 × 8·50 m, and 14·90 m high in centre.

30. Exterior from south-west.

31. Interior to east, with stucco decoration in gold and naturalistic colours on white, touches of blue-green in frieze, and some gold *mosaïque*, executed by Thomas Gering 1740–41; and large fresco of the Fountain of Life surrounded by small medallions of the Mysteries of the Rosary, signed and dated 1741, by Anton Endele (1700–61); altars (planned, 1736, by D. Z.) and pulpit executed by Ignaz Hillebrand, 1757–8, the side altars incorporating paintings of (s) the Holy Family with St Anne, 1747, and (N) the Deposition, 1752, both signed and dated by Endele.

32. Interior to west, with large fresco of the Coronation of the Virgin, smaller frescoes of (N) the Birth of the Virgin and (s) the Battle of Lepanto, and medallions of the Mysteries of the Rosary by Endele, 1741; small scagliola side altars; and nuns' choir.

33. Transverse section of choir.

34. Choir, with ceiling painting of the Virgin adoring the Christ Child by Endele; double altar, planned, 1736, by D. Z. and executed, 1757–8, by Hillebrand, incorporating a painting of the Three Kings by Paul Ignaz Viola (1727–1801), decorative carving by Ulrich Stengle, and additional figures at sides of Sts John Baptist and Joseph and the Agnus Dei over the tabernacle by Alois Egenberger, 1902 (!); and choirstalls, 1740–42, by Johann Michael Baur (1701–85).

Julius Schöttl, *Unser Lieben Frauen Kirche zu Günzburg a. D.*, (Augsburg, 1925).

Kunstführer 407, 4th ed., (Munich, 1957).

35. BUXHEIM (nr Memmingen), Carthusian Monastery. Annakapelle, built by D. Z., 1738–40, for Prior Georg Stock. Interior, with altar-piece of the Virgin with Sts Anne and Joachim signed by J. B. Z., white stucco decoration presumably by D. Z. rather than J. B. Z., and statues by (?) Sturm of Sts John Baptist, John Evangelist, Joseph and Judas Thaddeus, below, and Sts Barbara, Katherine, Agatha and Ursula, above. The ground in the vault is pale blue and the garlands gilded; some small areas on walls have blue and pink grounds and there are also touches of gold.

36. Annakapelle, vault.

Fritz Arens and Friedrich Stöhlker, *Die Kärtause Buxheim*, (Buxheim, 1962), pp. 22–3.

37. LANDSBERG, Johanniskirche. Designed and begun 1741; completed, 1750–52 (consecrated 1754), by D. Z. Façade, blue-grey with order in pale stone colour.

38. Scagliola altar by D. Z., designed 1741? or 1751?, incorporating Baptism of Christ by Johann Luidl with fresco behind by K. J. Thalheimer (1712–99). The porcelain tones of the scagliola are predominantly near-white and mottled pink.

Kunstführer 88, 2nd ed., (Munich, 1961), pp. 16–19.

39, 40. DIE WIES (nr Steingaden), Pilgrimage Church. Projected, *c*. 1743–4, for Abbot Hyazinth Gassner of the Premonstratensian Abbey of Steingaden and built, 1746–54 (choir consecrated 1749, nave consecrated 1754), by D. Z. for Abbot Marian II Mayr; with ceiling frescoes by J. B. Z. Final cost *c*. 180,000 gulden. Length 59·40m; nave 17·30m wide with aisles of 2m; height 20m to flat of ceiling.

Plans as projected and as executed.

41. Exterior from north, with Clergy House and Abbot's Summer Quarters to left. Yellow walls with white-painted orders and window frames, renewed in 1966, after this photograph was taken.

42. Interior to east, with stucco decoration, predominantly in white and gold with touches of pink, green, and gold *mosaïque*, and fresco of Judgement Throne by J. B. Z.; figures of Church Fathers by Sturm, *c*. 1753–4; and pulpit designed presumably by D. Z. and executed by Pontian Steinhauser and his sons (J. M., 1718–89, and F. X., 1735–1825).

43. Interior to west, with fresco of the Gate of Eternity and, below, the organ of 1756–7 by Andreas Jäger.

44. Interior to north, with altar executed, 1754–9, by Dominikus Bergmüller from D. Z.'s design, including Christ and the Magdalen painted by J. G. Bergmüller (1682–1762) flanked by wooden statues of the Magdalen and St Margaret of Cortona, with Abraham above, carved by Sturm.

45. Choir, 1746–9, with double altar enshrining, below, the Christ at the Column of 1730 (which is the principal object of devotion) and, above, a painting of the Holy Kin by B. A. Albrecht (1687–1765) in gold frame carved by (?) Sturm; and white stucco figures of the Four Evangelists and the Prophets Isaiah and Malachi completed, 1749, by Egÿd I Verhelst (1696–1749). Above is the Agnus Dei and, overhead, the fresco by J. B. Z. of angels carrying the Symbols of the Passion. Scagliola columns of galleries and body of altar mottled blue grey, altar columns mottled pink.

46. SCHUSSENRIED (nr Biberach), Premonstratensian Abbey. Wooden model made in 1749 of project by D. Z., 1748, for church and monastery for Abbot Siard Frick. (Now preserved in monastery library.) Partially executed with various modifications, 1752–63, by D. Z.'s former assistant Jakob Emele.

Kunstführer 163, 3rd. ed., (Munich, 1960).

47. ANDECHS (nr Starnberg), Benedictine Abbey and Pilgrimage Church. Built, 1425; restored, 1670–5, after fire; windows enlarged, 1712; drastically remodelled, omitting easternmost piers, 1751–5, by Lorenz Säppel (1705–59), with advice of Brother Ignaz Merani (1693–1762) and (presumably) of J. B. Z., for Abbot Bernhard Schütz; and restored 1938–40. Nave and choir 31·50 × 15·25 m.

Plan.

48. Interior to east, with stucco decorations in white, varied by highlights of gold and naturalistic tones on foliage, and ceiling fresco of Adoration of the Host, 1751–5, by J. B. Z. assisted by Josef Marian (†1755); red marble high altar, based on drawing of 1751 by J. B. Z., by F. X. Schmädl (1705–77), incorporating a fifteenth-century Madonna, and Angels, 1608–9, by Hans Degler (†1637); seventeenth-century figures of Sts Benedict and Scolastica and, forward on the balcony rail, Sts John Nepomuk and Florian by Schmädl; and side altars, c. 1755, by J. B. Straub (1704–84), including paintings, signed and dated 1703, by J. A. Wolff (1652–1716) of (N) the Death of St Benedict and (S) of St Rasso, flanked by figures of Sts Alphonsus and Anselm and Sts Bernard and Joseph, respectively, by Straub.

49. Drawing, now lost, of project for east end by J. B. Z., 1751.

50. Interior to west, with chronogram '1755' on balcony front.

Romuald Bauerreis and Hugo Schnell, *Der Heilige Berg Andechs*, (Munich, 1955).

Lieb, *Barockkirchen*, pp. 106–9, 161, 172 (Bibl. p. 161).

Kunstführer 394, 5th ed., (Munich 1960).

51. SCHÄFTLARN (nr Starnberg), Premonstratensian Abbey Church. Begun, 1733–40, by Cuvilliés, assisted by Franz Ronninger, for Abbot Melchior Schussmann; and completed with shortened transepts, 1751–6 (consecrated 1760), by J. B. Gunetzrhainer (1692–1763), assisted by 'Herr Fischer' – probably J. M. Fischer (1692–1766) – and Melchior Streicher (†1772), for Abbots Josef Frey and Felix Gege. Nave 30 × 20 m, presbytery 9·50×10·50 m, sanctuary 11×9·50 m; heights: nave 19 m, presbytery 16·60 m, sanctuary 16 m.

Interior to east, with stucco decoration in pink and putty colour on a white ground and frescoes of the Life of St Norbert and the History of Schäftlarn, 1754–6, by J. B. Z., assisted by his son F. M. Z.; high altar by J. B. Straub (†1784), 1755–6, incorporating an Assumption of the Virgin, signed and dated 1755, by B. A. Albrecht; and pulpit by Straub.

52. Interior to north, with one of the principal side altars by Straub including painting by Albrecht of Don Juan of Austria and Pius V before the Battle of Lepanto flanked by statues of Sts Dominick and Katherine of Siena by Straub; Straub's pulpit; and his altar of St Norbert.

Lieb, *Barockkirchen*, pp. 93–8, 159–60, 171 (Bibl. p. 160);
Kunstführer 537, (Munich, 1951).

53. NYMPHENBURG (nr Munich), Schloss. Festsaal. Inside the centre of the main block, which was begun in 1664 by Agostino Barelli (1627–c. 1680) and completed by Zuccalli ten years later for the Electress Henriette Adelheid; then remodelled according to later plans of Zuccalli by G. A. Viscardi (1645–1713), 1702–4, for the Elector Max Emanuel; again, 1720–22, by Effner for Max Emanuel; and finally by Cuvilliés, 1755–7, for the Elector Max III Joseph (1745–77).

Interior with gold and white stucco decorations and frescoes of Classical pastoral and hunting scenes – Cephalus and Procris in central panel – by J. B. Z., 1755–7, assisted by his son F. M. Z. (1709–84). J. B. Z.'s contract was for 2,800 florins for the frescoes; Lauro Bigarello's for the gilding was for 4,500–5,000 florins.

54. Music Gallery of Festsaal, with white stucco decoration executed from Cuvilliés's designs by J. B. Z. and F. M. Z., 1755–7, and ceiling fresco by J. B. Z. and F. M. Z.

Luisa Hager, *Nymphenburg*, (Munich, n.d.), pp. 57–60;
idem., *Nymphenburg*, (Konigstein-im-Taunus, 1964), pl. 11–15.

55. GUTENZELL (nr Biberach), Cistercian Nunnery Church. Built 1518; largely rebuilt 1647; design for remodelling provided, 1755–6, by D. Z. and carried out, probably by Nikolaus Rueff, for Abbesses Franciska von Gall and Maria Alexandra Zimmermann, D. Z.'s daughter. Length 58·50 m, including choir of 12·50 m; breadth 19 m, including aisles of 3 m; height of choir 18 m.

Interior, with stucco decoration by F. X. I. Feuchtmayr (1705–64) and his son-in-law Jakob Rauch; frescoes of Old Testament subjects on the ceiling and of the Twelve Apostles on the walls, 1756, by J. G. Dieffenbrunner (1718–86); pulpit, probably by Rauch though sometimes attributed to Ignaz Finsterwalder (1708–?); high altar from D. Z.'s design, dated 1763, carrying the Zimmermann arms above a painting of the Assumption of the Virgin dated 1692; and side altars of 1912. D. Z. received only 53 gulden 30 kreutzer for his original project; Rueff, 1199 gulden; and Feuchtmeyr, 1300 gulden.

Kunstführer 627, (Munich, 1955).

56. Project for 'constructed decoration' in choir, *c.* 1746–8. (Now preserved in museum at Weilheim [Haus Pfaffenwinkel]).

57. Choir gallery.

58. Fresco of Second Coming of Christ by J. B. Z. on ceiling of nave vignetted by white and gold stucco-work with touches of pink, blue-green, and gold *mosaïque.*

Lieb, *Barockkirchen*, pp. 118–28, 162–3, 172–3.

Carl Lamb, *Die Wies*, (Munich, 1964).

Index

Admout, Benedictine abbey library, 26

Albrecht, B.A., 28, 29, 58, 65, 75, 91, 93

Aldersbach, Augustinian monastery church, 28, 45, 57

Alsace, 47

Alteglofsheim, Schloss, 21, 60

Altenburg, Benedictine abbey library, 25

Altomünster, church, 82

Amigoni, Jacopo, 27, 28, 31, 40–43, 45, 52, 87

Ammersee, 32, 36, 64

Amsterdam, 22

Andechs, Benedictine abbey, 14, 32, 34, 35, 54, 74, 79, 80, 92, *plates* 47–50

Anglo-Palladian period, 17

Arens, Fritz, and Stöhlker, Friedrich, *Die Kartäuse Buxheim*, 85, 87, 91

Arlesheim, church, 36

Arolsen, 22

Asam, Cosmas Damian, 8*n*, 9, 25, 26, 28, 30, 31, 34, 41, 45, 46, 48, 52–3, 56–7, 60, 63–4, 79, 83

Asam, Egid Quiriu, 9, 22, 25, 26, 34, 41, 46, 48, 53, 63–4, 67, 79, 83

Asam Haus, Munich, 22, 23

atlantides, 42

Attel, Elandskapelle, 13

Attersee, 52

Augsburg, 22, 23, 27, 30, 37, 38, 70
    Akademie, 77
    Bishop of, 75
    Rathaus, 23

Augustinians, 20

Austria, 52

Baader, J. G., 41, 87

Bach, Johann Sebastian, 16

Bad Tölz, 25, 32, 87, 89

Baden-Baden, 22

Baden-Durlach, Margrave of, 22

Bader, Konstantin, 55

Baizin, Josefa, Prioress of Siessen, 47

Bamberg, 19, 22, 28

Barelli, Agostino, 93

Baroque, 7*ff*, 26*ff*
    Early, 26
    French, 8
    German, 7, 26–7
    Italian, 8, 27
    Late, 8, 26, 29, 67
    Northern, 8

Barthel, G., 84

Bauerreis, R., and Schnell, H., *Der Heilige Berg Andechs*, 92, *plate* 52

Baur, Johann Michael, 90

Bavaria, 16, 17, 28

Beer, Franz II, 47

Beich, F. J., 42, 87

Benedictines, 16, 20, 45, 56

Benediktbeuerne, Benedictine abbey of, 31, 35, 38, 50, 57, 61–2, 87, 89
    Anastasia kapelle, 81
    library, 12, 25, 31, 46, 55, 58, 87, *plate* 10
    Neuer Festsaal, 13, 56, 58, 87, *plate* 25

Berchtesgaden, Prince-abbot of, 18

Berg, duchy of, 20

Berg-am-Laim, church, 13, 68, 81

Bergmüller, Dominikus, 77, 91

Bergmüller, J. G., 24, 46, 77, 85, 91

Berlin, 27

Bernini, 26, 48, 70

Berntoff, Joseph Marquard von, 22

Beyharting, Augustinian abbey church, 13, 55, 58, 61

Biberach, pilgrimage church, 11, 35, 87

Bigarello, Lauro, 33, 93

Birkland, parish church, 12, 24

Birnau, pilgrimage church, 69

Black Forest, 26

Blenheim, battle of, 39

Blondel, François II, 57
Boffrand, Germain, 29, 39, 40, 49, 59–62
Bohemia, 49
boiserie(s), 40–42, 58, 60–62
Bonn, 23, 39
Borromini, 26, 48, 78
Bossi, Antonio, 27, 29
Bouchefort, 39, 40
Bourke, John, 16, 84
Bremen, 19
Brenner, Hans II, 86
Breslau, 38
Bruchsal, Schloss, 21
Bruford, W. H., 84
Brühl, Schloss Augustusburg, 21, 57, 61
Brussels, 39
Burrough, T. H. B., 84
Buxheim Carthusian monastery, 11, 13, 31, 33, 37, 55, 63, 85, 90, plates 2, 3
    Annakapelle, 13, 63, 67–8, 73–4, 76, 79, 90, plates 35–6
    library, 11, 25, 44
    Marienkapelle, 11, 38
    parish church, 12, 46–8, 51, 87, plates 11, 12
Byss, J. R., 28

Carl Albrecht, Elector of Bavaria, later Emperor Karl VII, 19, 28, 57, 59, 68–9, 89
Carl Ludwig, Elector Palatine, 39
Carthusians, 20, 63
Castelli, J. P., 29
Chiemsee, 24, 89
Cistercians, 20
Clemens August, Elector of Cologne, 20, 21, 23, 57, 59, 81
Clemenswerth, Schloss, 21
Cologne, 19, 20
Constance, 19
Correggio, 28
Cortona, Pietro da, 28, 56
Corvey, Prince-abbot of, 18
Cotte, Robert de, 39, 42, 43, 49, 86
Coypel, 28
Cuvilliés, François, 8, 16, 22, 25, 28, 29, 33, 53, 56–62, 73, 79, 81, 89, 92–3

Dachau, 39
Danube, 52
Deggendorf, 52
Degler, Hans, 92
Dehio, G., Handbücher der deutschen Kunstdenkmäler, 83; see also Gall, Ernst
Delamair, P. A., 59–60
Deutsch Orden, 20, 23, 41
Dieffenbrunner, J. G., 36, 94
Dientzenhofer, Christoph, 49
Dientzenhofer, Johann, 27
Diessen, Augustinian abbey, church, 64, 82
Dietramzell, Augustinian abbey, church, 12, 13, 31, 32, 55
    parish church, 31
Dietrich, Joachim, 58, 89

Dillingen, 7, 84
    Franciscan nuns' church, 66, 71
Dobler, Georg, 87
Dominicans, 20
Donauwörth, 32
Dossenbergers, 83
Dreifaltigkeitskirche, Munich, 14, 48
Dubut, Charles C., 40–43, 87
Düsseldorf, 17

Early Rococo, 71, 82
Ebersberg, Augustinians Monastery church, 72
Ebrach, Cistercian monastery, 38
Edelstetten, 44–5
    Frauenstift church, 11, 31, 38, 85, plate 1
Effner, Josef, 25, 28, 39–44, 52, 57–9, 81, 86–7, 93
Egenberger, Alois, 90
Einsiedeln, Benedictine abbey and pilgrimage church, 49, 53
Elisabeth Charlotte, duchesse d'Orléans ('Liselotte'), 39, 44
Ellingen, Rathaus, 20, 23, 41
Ellwangen, Prince-prior of, 18, 19
Emele, Jakob, 24, 26, 68, 78, 87, 92
Emmering, parish church, 13
Endele, Anton, 63, 90
England, 21, 22
English Georgian period, 17, 22
Eresing parish church, 14, 23, 36, 78
Esperlin, Josef, 88
Ettal, 33, 34
Ettenhofer, J. G., 72
Etwashausen, chapel, 29
Expressionism, 15

Faison, S. Lane, 83
Fatimà, 24
Feuchtmayr, F. X. I., 30, 36, 93, 94
Feuchtmayr, J. M., 82
Feulner, A., 60, 84
Finsterwalder, Ignaz, 94
Finsterwalder, Kaspar and Georg, 87
Fischer, J. G., 71
Fischer, J. M., 9, 16, 25, 30, 33, 34, 48, 62–4, 66, 68–9, 80–82, 83, 93
Fischer von Erlach, J. B., 48, 83
Fischingen, Benedictine abbey church, 11, 37
    Iddakapelle, 11, 37
Florence, 28
France, 24, 52
Francis of Lorraine, 69
Franciscans, see Dillingen; Günzburg; Ingolstadt
Franconia, 17, 19, 20, 28, 38
Franz I, Emperor, see Francis of Lorraine
Franz Georg von Schönborn, 19
Franz Ludwig, Elector of Trier, 41
Freising, 37
    Bishop of, 21
    Cathedral, 12, 28, 35, 37, 40, 46, 48, 53, 82
    library, 13, 25
    Neustift, 14, 33, 80
French Gothic, 15, 17
French Régence, 43
French Revolution, 18

French Rococo, 17, 26, 28, 38–42, 52, 55, 57
Frey, Abbot Josef, 93
Frick, Siard, Abbot of Schussenried, 47, 78, 92
Friedrich Carl, Prince-bishop of Bamberg and Würzburg, 19
Früholzer, Joachim, 32, 53–4, 88
Fuggers, 23
Fulda, cathedral of, 27
Functionalists, 51
Fürstenzell, Cistercian abbey church, 30

Gaibach, church, 66
Gall, Abbess Franciska von, 93
Gall, Ernst, *Handbuch der deutschen Kunstdenkmäler*, 83, 85, 86, 90
Gallery of Ancestors, *see* Munich Residenz,
Gassner, Abbot Hyazinth, 69–70, 75, 91
Gege, Abbot Felix, 93
George II, 17, 21
Gering, Thomas, 64, 90
German Rococo, *passim*; 8, 15, 17, 26, 79
Girard, Dominique, 40
Gombrich, E., 8
Gothic, French, 15, 17
grisaille, 73, 80
Groff, Willem de, 40
Grottenhof, 57
Guarini, 26, 49, 55
Gumpp, J. A., 40
Gunetzrhainer, J. B., 22, 56–7, 81, 92–3
Günther, E., 84
Günther, Ignaz, 33, 35, 89
Günzburg, Franciscan nunnery, 65; parish church, 13, 23, 24, 32, 34, 54, 63–6, 69–71, 73–4, 78–9, 90, *plates 29–34*
Gurlitt, Cornelius, 83
Gutenzell Cistercian nunnery church, 14, 35, 36, 54, 65, 78, 82, 92–3, *plate 55*

Habsburgs, 18
Hager, Luisa, *Nymphenburg*, 89, 93; *Schloss Schleissheim*, 87
Hainz, Josef, 44, 56, 87, 89
Hamburg, 19
Handel, G. F., 16
Hanover, 16
Harlass, Prior Gelasius, 88
Hauttmann, Max, 17, 84, 85
Hayberger, Gotthart, 25
Heilig-Kreuz Jesuit church, Landsberg, 34
Hempel, Eberhard, 7n, 84
Hennicke, Georg, 38
Henriette Adelheid, Electress of Bavaria, 93
Herkomer, J. J., 37, 38, 51
Hermann, F. G., 46, 87
Herrenchiemsee, Schloss, 15
Herrenhausen, Schloss, 16
Herrgottsruh, 30
Herzogsfreude, Schloss, 21

Heusenstamm, parish church, 29
Hieronymite(s), *see* St-Anna-am-Lehel, Munich
Hildebrandt, Johann Lukas von, 28, 41, 48, 64, 83
Hildesheim, Prince-bishop of, 20
Hillebrand, Ignaz, 32, 65, 90
Hitchcock, H.-R., 84
Hohenaschau, Schloss, 13, 22
Holl, Elias, 23
Holland, 21
Holzinger, F. J., 52, 53
Holzkirchen, Benedictine priory church, 29
Holy Roman Empire, 18
Hôtels, du Petit Luxembourg, 39, de Soubise, 59–60, de Toulouse, 43, 44, de Villars, 62
Huber, Brother Christian, 37

Industrial Revolution, 18
Ingenried, parish church, 13, 23, 69
Ingolstadt, Franciscan church, 13, 68, 81–2
Ingres, J.-A.-D., 8
International Style, 15
Ismaning, Schloss, 12, 21
Italy, 26, 52

Jäger, Andreas, 91
Johanniskirche, Landsberg, 13, 68, 73–4, 78, 91, *plates 37–8*
Joseph Clemens, Elector of Cologne, 20, 38, 39

Karl VI, Emperor, 63
Karl VII, Emperor, *see* Carl Albrecht
Karlskirche, Vienna, 48
Karlsruhe, 22
Kasper, Alfons, and Strache, Wolf, *Steinhausen*, 88
Kaufbeuren, 23
Kaufmann, Oskar, 15
Kempten, Prince-abbot of, 18, 63
Kidl, Georg Anton, 90
Kimball, Fiske, 8, 9, 27, 39, 43, 60, 62; *The Creation of the Rococo*, 84
Kitzingen, 29
Klenze, Leo von, 86
Köglsperger, P. J., 81
Königsfeld, Count von, 22
Köpf, Hans Michael, 87, 90
Kösingen, parish church, 12, 24
Krämer, Simpert, 38, 62, 85
Krepp, Johann Michael, 90
Kreuzpullach, parish church, 44
Kuen, F. M., 36, 51, 54, 88
Kumbach, 31

Lamb, Carl, 16, 74
    Die Wies, 92, *plates* 15, 29, 33, 39–40
Landsberg-am-Lech, 22, 23, 32, 34, 38, 63, 66, 78
    Ursuline (*now* Dominican) nunnery church (Ursulinerkirche), 12, 20, 46, 48
    parish church, 12
    Rathaus, 12, 23, 86, *plate* 7
Landshut, 32, 56, 68, 79
Late Baroque, *see* Baroque

Laugier, Abbé, 51, 82
Lawder, Standish D., 83
Le Brun, J., 43, 84
Le Corbusier, 24
Leikard, Prior Petrus, 85
Le Moyne, 28
Lepautre, Pierre, 39, 40, 82
Lespilliez, C. A. von, 22
Léveilly, Michel, 23
Lieb, Norbert, 69, 86, 88–9, 92–3,
    plate 24
Liebenburg, Schloss, 21
Liebert, 23
Liège, 18
London, 22
Lori, J. M., 75
Lori, Maria, 75, 77
Lothar Franz, Elector of Mainz, 19,
    28, 38
Lotz, Wolfgang, 72
Louis XIV, 21, 39, 40
Lower Saxony, 20
Lübeck, 19
Lucerne, Bürgerbibliotek, 87
Ludwig I of Bavaria, 86
Ludwig II of Bavaria, 15
Ludwigsburg, 22
    palace, 25
Ludwigskirche, Saarbrücken, 59
Luidl, Johann, 79, 91

Maderno, 48
Magges, Joseph, 77
Mainz, 19
Mannheim, 22, 25
Mansart, Jules Hardouin, 39
Mantegna, 28
Margarethenberg, 14
Maria Brunnlein, pilgrimage church,
    Wemding, 14, 32, 80
Maria Theresia, Empress 19, 69
Marian, Josef, 92
Märkl, Abbot Roman, 53
Marly, 39
Mascherino, 49
Max I of Bavaria, 86
Max Emanuel, Elector of Bavaria, 28,
    38–40, 44, 57, 86, 93
Max III Joseph, Elector of Bavaria,
    29, 33, 69, 93
Mayr, Marian II, Abbot of Stein-
    gaden, 69, 71, 91
Meissonier, J.-A., 62, 73, 79
Melk, Benedictine abbey library, 25
Memmingen, 25, 37, 85, 87
Merani, Brother Ignaz, 32, 34, 35, 92
Mergentheim, 20
Metten, Benedictine abbey church,
    52, 53, 72
    Festsaal, 71
Michelangelo, 8
Middle Ages, 17, 18, 20, 22
Miesbach, parish church, 12, 37
Mindera, Karl, Benediktbeuern, 87, 89
Miroffsky, Wenzel, 58
Mödingen, Dominican nunnery
    church, 12, 31, 46–8, 51, 54–5,
    65, 86 plates 5, 6
Mödlhammer, P., 89
Moosbrugger, Brother Kaspar, 49
Moretti, Pasqualin, 59

mosaïque, 45, 62, 66
Muchall-Viebrook, T., 84
Mungennast, Josef, 25
Munich, 22, 25, 35, 40, 44, 49, 52–3,
    64, 72, 81
    court, 58, 80
Munich Residenz, 41, 53, 56–7, 59,
    61–2, 87, 89
    Gallery of Ancestors (Ahnenga-
        lerie), 12, 28, 57–8, 65
    Grüne Galerie, 29, 57, 73
    Hofkapelle, 14, 79
    Reiche Zimmer, 13, 58, 62
    State Bedroom, 58
    Treasure Room (Schatzkammer,
        now Porzellankabinett), 13, 45,
        57–8, 89, plate 22
Münster, Prince-bishop of, 20

Neo-Classicism, 82
Neo-Rococo, 15
Neresheim, Benedictine abbey, 12, 24
Ness, Abbot Rupert II, 62, 86
Neumann, J. B., 9, 16, 24, 25, 27, 29,
    30, 34, 61, 64, 66, 69, 83
Neustift, see Freising
North Rhine-Westphalia, 20
Nymphenburg, Schloss, 14, 16, 25,
    29, 33, 80, 82, 89, 93
    Amalienburg, 8, 13, 16, 27, 57–62,
        68, 89, plate 26
    Badenburg pavilion, 13, 40–42, 44
    Chorfrauenkirche, 13, 57, 59
    Great Hall (Festsaal), 29, 33, 79,
        80, 93, plate 53
    Magdalenenklause, 59
    Mirror Room (Spiegelsaal), 16,
        59–61, 73, 89, plate 25
    Music Gallery, 93, plate 54
    Pagodenburg, 39–42

Oberammergau, parish church, 33
Obořiště, 49
Ochsenhausen, Benedictine abbey, 12
Oppenord, G.-M., 39
Osnabrück, Prince-bishop of, 20
Ötschmann, Michael, 31, 44, 56, 87,
    89
Ottobeuren, Benedictine abbey, 11–
    13, 25–6, 64, 69, 81–2, 85–6
    church, 16, 30, 40, 62, 89, plate 24
    library, 12, 25, 31, 40, 44, 86,
        plate 4

Pachinger, Abbot Magnus, 44, 87, 89
Pagodenburg, see Nymphenburg
Palais Daun-Kinsky, 41; Holnstein,
    13; Piosasque de Non, 57;
    Porcia, 13; Preysing, 12, 22
Palais Royal, Galerie d'Oppenord, 44,
    71
Paris, 17, 22, 28, 29, 43, 57–62
Passau, 28
Philippe II, duc d'Orléans, 44
Pichler, J. A., 40, 41, 42
Piedmontese Baroque, 26
pilgrimage churches, 20, 24, 32, 71
    see also under individual churches
    e.g. Biberach; Einsiedeln; Brunn-
        lein; Steinhausen; Vierzehnhei-
        ligen; Vilgertshofen

Pineau, Nicolas, 62
Polling, 71
Pommersfelden, Schloss Weissenstein, 21, 28, 38, 41
Pöring, Schloss, 22, 66, 68
Portugal, 24
Powell, Nicolas, 8, 84
Pozzo, Andrea, 27
Prague, 31
Prandtauer, Jakob, 25–6
Premonstratensian(s), 16, 20, 24, 76, 80; see also Frick, Siard; Schäftlarn; Schussenried; Steingaden; Ströbele, Didacus
Prestel, J. G., 88
Preysings, 22; see also Hohenaschau, Schloss; Palais Preysing
Prien, parish church, 13, 24, 31, 62, 65–6, 68, 71, 89, plates 27–8
prince-abbots, 18, 63
prince-bishops, 18–21
prince-prior, 18, 19
Pugin, 51

Rainaldi, 48
Raitenhaslach, church, 35
Rastatt, 22
    Treaty of, 39
Rauch, Jakob, 23, 36, 93–4
Regensburg, 22, 26, 36, 60, 64
Renaissance, 15, 17, 22, 25, 34
Residenz Theater, Munich (now Cuvilliés Theater), 14, 80, 81
Reusch, J. G., 85, 88
rocaille, 33, 73–7, 79–82
Rohr, Augustinian monastery church, 67
Rohrmoser, Justina, 37
Roman High Baroque, 26
Romanesque, 17, 35
Romantic Classicism, 17
Rome, 27, 28, 48, 49, 56, 70, 78
Ronchamp, 24
Ronninger, Franz, 81, 92
Roth, F. J., 23, 32, 41, 80
Rott-am-Inn, Benedictine abbey church, 63
Rottmayr, J. F. M., 28, 45
Rueff, Nikolaus, 36, 93
Rupprecht, B., 84
Rusch, 52
Russia, 62

St-Anna, Munich-Harlaching, 14
St-Anna (Damenstiftskirche), Munich, 57
St-Anna-am-Lehel, Munich, 48–9, 64
Sant' Anna dei Palafrenieri, Rome, 48
Sankt Blasien, Benedictine monastery church, 13
St-Blasius, Dominican church, Landshut, 13, 14, 32, 68, 79
St. Cloud, 39
St-Egidius, Nürnberg, 44
St-Florian, Augustinian monastery library, 25–6
St-Jakob-am-Anger, Munich, 13
St-Johann-Nepomuk, Munich, 64
St-Kassian, Regensburg, 36
St-Mang, church, Füssen, 37
St-Paulinus, Trier, 29

Sankt Peter, monastery church, 26, 34
St-Peter church, Munich, 14, 79
Salesian Brothers, 44, 56, 87
Salzburg, 18, 48
Sankt Gallen, monastery library, 26
Säppel, Lorenz, 32, 34, 35, 92
scagliola (Stuckmarmor) altars, 11–14, 23, 30, 33, 35, 37, 54, 75, 79, 85, 88–9, 91
    columns, 67, 74, 86–7
    intarsia, 41
    pulpit, 90
    walls, 87
Schäffler, Christoph, 37
Schäftlarn, Premonstratensian Abbey church, 14, 33, 53, 80–82, 92–3, plates 51–2
Schalk, Sigmund, 85
Schäzler Haus, Augsburg, 22
Scheffler, C. T., 29
Schenk, Daniel, 38, 40
Schlaun, J. C., 57
Schleissheim, Neues Schloss, 12, 25, 28, 38–41, 45, 52, 55, 58–9, 61, 86–7
    Great Hall (Festsaal), 12, 31, 42–4, 50, 52, 86, plate 8
    Hall of Victories (Viktoriensaal), 42
    Kammerkapelle, 12, 41, 43–6, 87, plate 9
    Maximiliankappele, 12, 31
    Stairhall, 12
    Writing Room, 41, 44
Schliersee, parish church, 11
Schlüter, Andreas, 40
Schmädl, F. X., 92
Schmid, J. B., 84
Schmuzer, Franz Xaver I, 9n, 23
Schmuzer, Franz Xaver II, 9n, 24
Schmuzer, Johann, 9n, 37, 38, 65
Schmuzer, Joseph, 9n, 30, 33, 37
Schnell, Hugo, Ottobeuren, 86
Schnell, H. M., 84
Schönborns, 19–21, 24; see also Lothar Franz
Schongau, parish church, 14, 23, 68, 73
Schörfling, 52
Schöttl, Benedikt, 52, 71
Schöttl, Julius, 86, 90
Schussenried, Premonstratensian abbey, 14, 68, 73, 78, 92, plate 46
    abbot(s) of, 24; see also Frick, S.; Ströbele, D.
    library, 26
Schussmann, Abbot Melchior, 92
Schütz, Abbot Bernhard, 32, 92
Schütz, Nikolaus, 36, 88
Schwäbisch-Gmünd
    Dominican monastery church, 12, 46, 48
    Franciscan church, 14
Sciascia, Lorenzo, 35, 55, 88
Seligenthal, Landshut, Cistercian nunnery church, 13, 56, 65, 81
Siessen, Dominican nunnery church, 12, 30, 46–8, 51, 54–5, 57, 62, 65,
Sitwell, Sacheverell, 7, 16, 84
Sondergotik, 17, 72
Speyer, 19

Stein zu Rechtenstein, von, Prioress Magdalena, 86
Steingaden, Premonstratensian abbey, 24, 69, 91
  Abbot of, 23; *see also* Gassner, H.; Mayr, Marian II
Steinhausen, pilgrimage church, 7–8, 12, 24, 29, 31, 32, 46–56, 58, 60–73, 75–80, 82, 87–8, *plates* 13–20
Steinhauser, Pontian, 77, 87, 90–91
Steinpeisz, Johann, 31, 66, 89
Stengel, F. J., 59
Stengle, Ulrich, 32, 90
Sterzing, 53
Stock, Prior Georg, 90
Strasbourg, 18
Straub, J. B., 82, 92, 93
Straubing, 52
Streicher, Melchior, 93
Ströbele, Didacus, Abbot of Schussenried, 47, 87
Stuber, N. G., 87
Sturm, Anton, 67–8, 72–3, 75, 77, 86–7, 90–91
Sufermeister, P., 84
Swabia, 17
Switzerland, 26, 36, 37, 49

Tegernsee, Benedictine monastery, 11, 12, 37
Thalheimer, Arbogast, 86
Thalheimer, K. J., 79, 91
Thirty Years' War, 17, 21, 36
Thoma, Hans, *Residenzmuseum München*, 89
Thon, C., 84
Thumb, Peter II, 9n, 26, 34, 69
Thurgau, Canton, 37
Tiepolo, G. B., 16, 27, 29, 35
Trent, 18, 27
Trost, Gottlieb, 44
Turin, 52
Tyrol, 53

Übelherr, J. G., 33
Ulm, 26
Untersteiner, J. B., 88
Ursulines (*now* Dominican nuns), *see* Landsberg

Vassé, F.-A., 43
Venice, 45
Verhelst, Egÿd I, 58, 75, 91
Versailles, 15, 21, 22, 25, 28, 43
  Grand Trianon, 39
  Ménagerie, 39
Vienna, 19, 27, 28, 41, 48
Vierzehnheiligen, pilgrimage church, 69
Vignola, 48, 49
Vilgertshofen, pilgrimage church, 13, 65, 71
Viola, Paul Ignaz, 90
Viscardi, G. A., 33, 40, 52, 72, 80, 93
Vittone, B.A., 26
Vogt, Father Christoph, 31, 38, 85–6
Volterra, Francesco da, 48

Waldeck and Pyrmont, Prince of, 19
Waldsee, Augustinian abbey church, 11, 31, 38

War of the Austrian Succession, 23, 69, 78, 81
War of the Spanish Succession, 39
Waräthi, Innozenz, 53, 72
Wasserburg-am-Inn, 23
Wertheim, 37, 74, 92
Weingarten, Benedictine abbey church, 51, 56
Weis, G. D., 87
Weissenstein, Schloss, 28, 31, 38, 41
Welsch, Maximilian von, 49
Weltenburg, 26, 41, 48, 63–4
Wemding, 32, 80, 82, parish church 11, 24; *see also* Maria Brunnlein
Werneck, Schloss, 21, 27, 29
Wessobrunn, 65
Wessobrunn-Gaispoint, 37
Westphalia, 17
Weyarn, Augustinian abbey church of, 12, 35, 55–6, 58, 61, 88–9, *plate* 21
Wiblingen, Benedictine abbey library, 26
Wiedemann, Christian, 26
Wiedemann, Johann, 26
Wies, Die, pilgrimage church, 7, 8, 13, 16, 23, 24, 27, 29, 32, 34, 49, 51, 53, 54, 62–3, 65, 68–79, 82, 91–2, *plates* 39–45, 56–8
William II, 15
Wittelsbachs, 19, 20, 21, 23, 25
Wolfegg, church, 71
Wolff, J. A., 92
Worms, 19
Worobiow, N., 84
Wright, Frank Lloyd, 8
Württemberg, 20, 22, 24, 31
Würzburg, 19
  Kapelle, 30
  Neumünster, 12, 13, 49, 56
  Residenz, 16, 62
  chapel (Hofkirche) (Sala terrena), 49, 64
  Garden Room, 35
  Kaisersaal, 27, 29
  Stairhall, 27
  Weisser Saal, 27, 61

Zeiller, J. J., 33
Zick, Johann, 35
Zimmermann, Dominikus, *see under individual works*
Zimmermann, Elias, 37
Zimmermann, Franz Dominikus, 77, 83
Zimmermann, Franz Michael, 33, 80, 87, 93
Zimmermann, Georg (*later* Father Thaddäus), 24, 78
Zimmermann, Johann Baptist, *see under individual works*
Zimmermann, Joseph, 87, 89
Zimmermann, Maria Alexandra (*later* Abbess of Gutenzell), 36, 78, 93
Zobel, Elias, 31, 84
Zöpf, Therese, 37
Zöpf, Thomas, 37
Zuccalli, Enrico, 33, 40, 41, 44, 57, 86, 93
Zwiefalten, Benedictine monastery church, 30, 69, 82, Abbot of, 63